A Philosophy of Israel Education

D1599963

Barry Chazan

A Philosophy of Israel Education

A Relational Approach

palgrave
macmillan

Barry Chazan
Hebrew University of Jerusalem
Spertus Institute of Jewish Learning and
Lincolnshire, Illinois, USA

ISBN 978-3-319-30778-7   ISBN 978-3-319-30779-4   (eBook)
DOI 10.1007/978-3-319-30779-4

Library of Congress Control Number: 2016945369

Cover illustration: © Melisa Hasan

Printed on acid-free paper

This Palgrave Macmillan imprint is published by Springer Nature
The registered company is Springer International Publishing AG Switzerland

CONTENTS

ABOUT THE AUTHOR

Barry Chazan is Professor Emeritus of the Hebrew University of Jerusalem and teaches at the Spertus Institute of Jewish Learning and Leadership.

1

A Relational Philosophy of Israel Education

Abstract Twenty-first-century Jewish life requires a new paradigm for Israel education that remains loyal to the past, but speaks to today and tomorrow. The purpose of this book is to respond to this challenge by presenting a new approach denoted as "a relational philosophy of Israel education". The chapter analyzes the meanings of ten terms that will appear throughout the book, and then presents eight principles of a relational philosophy of Israel education.

Keywords Cognitive emotions • Ethnic education • Homeland • Jewish identity • Narratives • Relational education

Our Task

What a complicated life this little land has lived. It has been *terra sancta* to great religions. It has endured multiple conquerors and occupiers. It has been the object of holy memory and vision of return. It is a modern state which is part of the family of nations. It is a source of conflicting aspirations and emotions. What a complicated life this little land lives.

This book is about the place of the Land of Israel in the educational system of contemporary American Jewish education. The Jewish preoccupation with Israel did not begin in the twentieth century. The land, people, and idea of Israel have been an integral part of Jewish life and education throughout the ages (Hartman 1978; Hoffman 1986). Twentieth-century American Jewish life perpetuated this connection

© The Author(s) 2016
B. Chazan, *A Philosophy of Israel Education*,
DOI 10.1007/978-3-319-30779-4_1

1

to Israel, even as it focused on the primary agenda of Americanization (Sarna 2004). The diverse educational systems of American Jewry taught about both the historical homeland and the newly created state established in 1948 (Chazan 2015). While America's Jews focused on becoming Americans, they also wanted their young to learn about the newly created state.

The twenty-first century is a different place. Jews are fully at home in, and constitute a robust part of, American life. Twentieth-first-century America is populated by a generation of post-ethnic multi-identified millennials (Hollinger 2000). The once pioneering State of Israel is now a powerful post-modern country located in a complex area of the world. These changes have significant implications for the relationship between American Jewry and Israel (Beinart 2000). The prior Jewish agenda of community and continuity has been replaced by a millennial agenda of multiple Jewish identities, the search for meaning, and the creation of affiliations of shared meaning (Magid 2013). This new situation calls for a new Israel educational paradigm that remains loyal to the past, but is relevant to the realities of today and tomorrow. That is the purpose of this book: to create a twenty-first century philosophy of Israel education.

This reconceptualization reaffirms the centuries-long Jewish commitment to the concept of Israel. At the same time it presents a new educational theory rooted in a vision of Israel education, as education for character and *humanitas* rather than ethnicity and particularism. The vision to be presented in this book focuses on relating and relationship rather than "we" versus "they" (Eriksen 2002; Buber 1934; Noddings 1992). Our work is rooted in the analytic approach to philosophy of education which views the elucidation of common language as critical for educational discourse and practice (Scheffler 1960; Soltis 1978). We also draw upon research and scholarship from philosophy, history, sociology, and education studies to enable us to propose a new educational theory and practice. Chapter 1 of the book presents the core principles of "A Relational Philosophy of Israel Education". Chapter 2 focuses on the translation of this philosophy of Israel education into educational practice. Chapter 3 focuses on the creation of a culture of Israel education and the role of Israel educator. The Epilogue is a meditation on the implications of this study of Israel in American Jewish education for an overall vision of ethnic education as ethical education.

Establishing a Language

We begin by analyzing certain key concepts which are important for understanding the relational philosophy of Israel education presented in this book.

Cognitive Emotions

Typically, cognition and emotion have been regarded as polar opposites. Cognition is regarded as sober, calm, reflective, and detached, while emotion is regarded as passionate, turbulent, heart-felt, and engaged. Cognition is understood as a faculty of the mind by which we analyze things in a "sensible" way, whereas emotion is regarded as a faculty of the heart whereby we feel things with "great sensitivity". In a significant essay entitled "In Praise of the Cognitive Emotions", the American analytic philosopher of education Israel Scheffler rejects the separation of the concepts "the cognitive" and "the emotive", and instead presents the case for their inherent interaction. He proposes "to help overcome the gap by outlining basic aspects of emotion in the cognitive process" (Scheffler 1991, p. 3). His purpose is to show that cognition incorporates emotional components and together they create "cognitive significance". This concept of cognitive emotions has important implications for the approach to Israel education that we shall discuss in Chaps. 2 and 3.

Ethnic Education

The field of ethnic education (and a subdivision sometimes called ethno-cultural education) emerged in the USA in the 1960s and 1970s as a result of both the mid-twentieth-century interest in the diverse groups that comprised American society as well as the impact of the Civil Rights Movement (Banks 1987). In its original iterations, the field of ethnic education focused on teaching and learning about the diverse immigrant heritages that comprised the panorama of American immigration. Over time, the agenda of ethnic education changed its focus. Toward the end of the century, it focused on political and ideological issues of race, gender, colonialism, and education, creating, what became known as, "identity politics" (Hollinger 2000). In the twenty-first century, this field focuses on multi-cuturalism and on, what is now called, the post-ethnic age

(Hollinger 2000). Israel education has encompassed some characteristics that seemed similar to contemporary ethnic education (such as language and culture) and, therefore, it sometimes has been regarded as part of that genre. At the same time, it is not adequately represented by that term, and, therefore, we shall use the formulation of the distinguished American educational historian Lawrence Cremin, who describes Jewish education as an "ethno-religious educational heritage" (Cremin 1988).

Homeland

The word "homeland" is a significant concept in the language of ethnicity and ethnic education. Typically, the term refers to a land (or an area), which is the place of origin of people and its culture, as well as the locus of a culture's history, language, customs, foods, and literary and artistic creations (Banks 2012).[1] In twentieth-century America, the term "homeland" was associated with places from which millions of immigrants arrived. It was scrapbooks with photographs and memories; dinner tables of exotic and enticing cuisine; and the language one used when you didn't want the children to understand (Daniels 1990). America itself was not "homeland"; it was the home of immigrants from diverse homelands.[2] "Homeland" becomes an Americanized concept at the end of the twentieth century, and especially after 9/11 when it became associated with terrorism and security on homeland American shores.[3] We shall focus on both home and homeland in discussing Israel education.

Identity

The word "identity" became popular in mid-twentieth-century America through the writings and teachings of Erik Erikson (Friedman 1999).[4] In his early formulations, Erikson used the term "identity" to refer to one of eight stages in psychosocial development (Erikson 1950). According to this typology, there are a series of lifelong developmental stages which involve a series of epigenetic "crises" whose resolution leads to the emergence of strengths important for a balanced and satisfying life. The psychosocial crisis of the fifth stage ("adolescence") is "identity versus identity confusion" in which identity refers to a person's shaping a psychological sense of who she/he is. The optimal outcome of the stage of identity confusion is the virtue of fidelity. Thus, identity in its original usage was very much about an activity and a process which plays out over time; Erikson went on to later describe it as a feeling of being "most deeply and intensely active and alive" (Friedman 1999, p. 351).[5] Erikson most decidedly did not refer to identity as loyalty to a specific ideology or group, nor did he regard it as a "subject" to be taught in schools. We shall refer to the metamorphosis of the original psychological meaning of "identity" to its current usage in Jewish life to mean loyalty or affirmation.

Israel

The word "Israel" (*Yisrael* in Hebrew) was first used in the Bible in the *Book of Genesis,* Chap. 28, Verse 22, when the name of the biblical figure Jacob was changed to "Israel" after a long night of wrestling with an angel of God.[6] Subsequently, the word became attached to the heretofore nameless land promised to Abraham which became *Eretz Yisrael* (the Land of Israel). The "Land of Israel" became the term used to describe this particular land, and its inhabitants became known as *B'nai Yisrael*—sons of Israel, children of Israel, or simply Israelites[7] (Alter 1990). In the period of the Israelite monarchy (beginning approximately in the eleventh century BCE), the Northern Kingdom composed of ten tribes, was denoted by the single word "Israel" and the two southern tribes were called "Judea" (Bright 1960). In post-Temple times (after 70 CE), the word "Israel" was used in diverse constellations such as *Eretz Yisrael* (the land), *Am Yisrael* (The Jewish people), *Torat Yisrael* (the Torah of Israel), and even *Elohei Yisrael* (The God of Israel). In later centuries, Jews in some Western or Central European countries were sometimes referred to as Israelite congregations.[8] In 1948, when the new Jewish State was established, Israel was the name chosen for the country (Friling and Troen 1998). Overall, the people known as the Jews have been connected over the ages to "Israel" and one of our tasks is to explicate the implications of this connection for Israel education (Hartman 1978).

Teaching Israel

For most of the past century, the phrase used to describe the school-based educational activity related to Israel was "Teaching Israel" (Chazan 2015). This phrase referred to a topic called Israel which was one of several topics taught in Jewish day and supplementary schools. This subject encompassed diverse topics such as the biblical Land of Israel; the ongoing link to Israel in prayers, rituals, and customs; the nascent Zionist movement, the founding of the state, and contemporary Israel (Essrig and Segal 1966).

The topic was approached through diverse frames, namely, historical, religious, ritual, and contemporary. The phrase "Teaching Israel" assumed a content- or subject matter-focused approach linked to school frameworks. Toward the end of the twentieth century, several voices called for replacing this terminology with the phrase "Israel education" which was understood as referring to a value-oriented vision and to broadening the educational frameworks beyond schools (*The Aleph Bet of Israel Education, 2nd Edition* 2015).[9] This book is about creating a twenty-first-century theory and practice of the term "Israel education".

Jewish Education

The term "Jewish education" is typically used to refer to the network of supplementary schools, day schools, camps, youth movements, and other educational frameworks which constitute a full-fledged system developed by twentieth-century American Jewry (Woocher and Woocher 2014; Graff 2013). Since the middle of the past century, this system has usually been categorized as religious education since schools were generally attached to denominational synagogues. It is difficult to neatly categorize Jewish education as "religious" since, while it does include faith-based elements, it also encompasses language, culture, foods, and a deep attachment to the State of Israel. Therefore, once again we shall understand Jewish education in Cremin's terms as an ethno-religious heritage.

Narratives

Narratives are ways of looking at the world, typically embedded in stories, which reflect how a person or group of individuals understand empirical facts and turn them into frameworks for making sense out of life. The various meanings of Israel have been embedded in narratives constructed by Jews at different points in time—biblical, rabbinic, modern, Zionist, contemporary statehood, and peoplehood—to help them make sense of the Land of Israel in diverse eras. A variety of distinctive narratives of the meaning of Israel developed over time, reflecting a core commitment to the overall idea, although expressed in divergent contents. There have also been diverse non-Jewish narratives—Christian, Muslim, and Palestinian—that reflect dramatically different understandings and interpretations of facts and events. Narratives will play an important role in the pedagogy of a relational Israel education.

Relational Education

"Relational education" is a term connected to a long, educational tradition which believes that the ultimate focus in education is on the kind of life a person leads and the core values which shape that life. This tradition, which dates back to Hellenistic and Hebraic times, believes that we must learn how to be human, and that education plays an important role in that quest. The philosophic approach to Israel education presented in this book is in that tradition. We focus on the place of Israel in personal growth and development. Our approach is dialogic in the sense that it regards the relationship of the individual to Israel as the subject of Israel education (Buber 1934). It is person-centered in that it regards the individual as an indispensable partner in the educational process (Rogers 1969; Dewey 1938; Aristotle 1966). It is present-oriented in its belief that education is not preparation for some far-off time called adulthood, but rather it is for how we live in the here and now (Korczak 2007; Dewey 1938). This approach is essentialist in the sense that it is committed to the critical role of ideas, knowledge, and contents in education. It is constructivist in its belief that understanding can only be realized when the individual is an active partner in the creation of knowledge. It is difficult to delineate one precise term that encompasses all these components. We shall use the phrase "relational education" to emphasize the significant role of the interaction of the student with values, a place, a history, and a people denoted by the word "Israel".

EIGHT PRINCIPLES OF A RELATIONAL APPROACH TO ISRAEL EDUCATION

Relational Israel education is rooted in eight educational principles, which have decisive implications for educational practice.

The first principle is that the individual—not Israel—is the center of Israel education. This principle indicates that the learner is the pivot or axis around which education revolves and for which education exists. This is not to say that the word "Israel" is insignificant, but it is not the starting point of Israel education—the learner is. While starting with Israel is tempting because it highlights an important topic, this direction usually leads to preoccupation with Israel and neglect of the student. The person-centered assumption is rooted in the moral and epistemological belief that people of all ages can think and feel, and that understanding is a process that takes place at all stages of development. Therefore, the focus of education should be on the person's thinking, feeling, and doing. Jerome Bruner said that any child could be taught any subject at any age (Bruner 1960). Jean Piaget hypothesized that children are young scientists who actively try to explore the world and make sense of it (Piaget 1969). Lawrence Kohlberg suggested that children are moral philosophers who confront moral issues according to a series of well-defined developmental levels (Kohlberg 1980). Nel Noddings said that children can be taught to care (Noddings 1992). Contemporary evolutionary psychologists and neuroscientists talk about "the moral sense", "the philosophical baby", "the ethical brain", and "the moral animal" (Alison Gopnik 2009; Michael Gazzaniga 2005; James Wilson 1993; Robert Wright 1994). These diverse sources are not simply romantic meditations or wishful thinking; they are increasingly verifiable findings about the central role of the learner as the focus of education. If educators presume that the young can reflect and think, then they will likely discover that students can reflect and think. If educators presume that the young are furnitureless rooms, then they will continue to see their jobs as interior decorators. The relational approach to Israel education begins with the belief that the child is the starting point on the exciting journey of Israel education.

The second principle of the relational approach is that the content of Israel education is the individual's relationship with Israel. The word "subject" is generally used in education to refer to the content or body of knowledge to be taught. Typically, the "subject" of Israel education has been defined as the history of Israel, the religious value of Israel, and the story of contemporary State of Israel, which are regarded as bodies of knowledge to be transmitted to the young. Our second principle says that these topics are not the subject, but rather they all come to serve the more central preoccupation with the development of a personal and interpersonal relationship with Israel. This principle is based on the assumption that human life is interactional and relational, and is dependent on connections with other ideas, values, beliefs, and people. It proposes that the intent of Israel education is about initiating, igniting, and nurturing a personal and hopefully long-lasting connection with Israel as it focuses on value, place, historical theme, contemporary state, and people. The creation of the relationship, rather than the memorization of a definable quantity of material, is the subject of Israel education.

The third principle proposes that the aim of Israel education is the exploration of core ideas related to the concept of Israel as being part of the larger enterprise of developing and creating a personal relationship with Israel. It regards the explication and understanding of diverse Israel narratives as important for a person's journey toward the goal of making meaning out of Israel. This goal statement is rooted in an educational tradition defined alternatively as humanistic, liberal, progressive, or person-centered education (Aristotle 1966; Dewey 1938; Frankl 1959; Oakshott 1989; Rogers 1980). This principle implies that understanding Israel can lead to a sense of lineage with a past heritage, linkage with a contemporary like-minded group of people, and inner harmony with one's self. We use the phrase "meaning making" to indicate that the pursuit of meaning is not frivolous, fleeting, or irrational, but, rather, it is an activity in which one has to work seriously (Freud 1900). Meaning doesn't just happen; it involves the dynamics of searching, considering, and reflecting. It is work, and takes time and effort. Moreover, meaning is not a subject to be taught in school, but, rather, it is a state of mind and heart that hopefully will emerge in the process of education.

The fourth principle is that along with understanding, meaning making, and relating, the creation of an Israel culture is a primary pedagogic focus of Israel education. The culturalist theory is a perspective which emphasizes the significant role of environment and context, for example, language, aesthetics, arts, food, and customs in education (Bruner 1999; Vygotsky 1978; Cole 1996). The cultures we live in are profound factors in shaping shape mind, self:

> Learning and thinking are always situated in a cultural setting and always dependent on the use of cultural resources... Culturalism takes as its first premise that education is not an island but part of the continent of culture. (Bruner 1999)

This means that Israel education includes the shaping of an immersive environment which encompasses the architecture, the peer culture, the hidden curriculum, teacher personality, weather, and other components that constitute the venue in which people learn. The architectonics of Israel education go beyond the formal course of study and include a much broader palate of educational opportunity. This means that the totality of educational institutions can be harnessed for Israel education.

The fifth principle of relational Israel education is that there is a rich corpus of diverse Israel narratives that are part of the Jewish heritage, which should be encountered and introduced in the context of Israel education. These narratives reflect diverse ways of looking at the world that have been created within the context of the Jewish experience. The tasks of Israel education in this instance are fourfold. The first task is to help the learner to understand that the Jewish people have retained an overall commitment to the Land of Israel as one of its core values. The second task is to enable the learner to discover that diverse meanings and understandings of Israel have been part of Jewish life over the ages. The third task of narrative teaching is to enable the learner to understand that the multiplicity of Israel narratives reflects a tradition which invites reflection, interpretation, and understanding of changing environments in which Jews have lived. The fact that contemporary Israel is a particularly charged topic does not mean that teachers or students must leave their cognitive skill sets in the locker room when dealing with this topic. They must approach it with the same cognition and passion that they utilize in approaching any serious question. The final task of narrative teaching is to help the young develop the skill sets which will enable them, at some point, to carve out their own personal Israel narrative. Ultimately, Israel education is about the internalization of virtues of intellectual honesty, curiosity, integrity, and commitment which are critical for making us human.

The sixth principle of person-centered Israel education is that good Israel education happens when there is connectivity between vision, proximate aim, content, and pedagogy. Such connectivity or "consilience" is reflected in the Athenian Greek notion of *paideia* or the Jewish notion of *Talmud Torah* in which a core educational vision shaped the totality of society and life (Jaeger 1944). The more an educational system can establish coordination between vision, educational theory, and practice, the greater the possibilities of impact. Developing a practice of Israel education is definitely not an activity of seeking "good programs that work". The integration of the diverse components of the educative process is a desideratum of Israel education. Such an approach aspires to create an educational symphony which both artfully and intelligently creates music and which sings to the hearts and minds of the young.

The seventh principle of relational Israel education is that it requires pedagogues who understand the overall vision, have the ability to make Israel narratives accessible to the student, can shape cultures, and have the courage to be accessible models and to teach "from within" (Palmer 1998). Understanding the vision means familiarity with the narratives of Israel that are the heritage of the Jewish people. Having the ability to make these narratives accessible encompasses skills in relationship-building, questioning, and group dynamics. Shaping cultures means to create environments which teach by immersing the student in an environment which "breathes" Israel. "Teaching from within" refers to the willingness to reach into one's self and to model one's Israel relationship (and its complexities) with love and passion. Those best suited to engage in Israel education are people who co-opt their personal passion and questions in order to model a commitment that is human, but not uncritical.

The eighth principle of a relational Israel education is the recognition of the power and the limits of education. Emile Durkheim saw education as all-powerful, and he warned teachers of the frightening power they had as transmitters of society (Durkheim 1956). Sigmund Freud mused on the near-impossible and futile task of teaching in the face of the overwhelming constraints of civilization (Britzman 2009). The truth lies somewhere between Durkheim and Freud. Education—and Israel education—can make a difference and may well contribute to a meaningful Israel relationship. At the same time, we should not forget the plethora of other forces—genetics, family, media, cyberspace, life's twists, and turns, which play such a significant role in shaping who we will become. Israel education is not the answer, the solution, or the magic bullet, but Israel educators are entrusted with the opportunity to be a force that matters. Israel education may be a Sisyphus-like activity; yet, we continue to try to roll the stone up the mountain. And there are times when we succeed (Bernfeld 1973).

So what is Israel education according to the relational approach? It is the exhilarating and the humbling mission of educating people to think, feel, and integrate Israel into their overall character as Jews and as human beings. It is about the attempt to help young Jews study their particular culture in an attempt to find meaning in a place, an idea, a people, and a value that has been dear to their tradition. It is about helping people seek answers to life's most basic questions through the portal of one's particular tradition.

BIBLIOGRAPHY

Alter, R. (1990). *The five books of Moses*. New York: W. W. Norton and Company, 2004. Print.

Alter, Robert. (1994). *Hebrew and Modernity*. Bloomington: Indiana UP. Print.

Aristotle, and W.D. Ross. (1966). *The Works of Aristotle*. London: Oxford U. Print.

Banks, J. (1987). *Multi-cultural education*. Boston: Allyn and Bacon.

Banks, J., & McGee Banks, C. A. (2012). *Multi-education: Issues and perspectives*. New York: Wiley, 2012. Print.

Banks, James and Cherry A. McGee Banks. (2013). *Multicultural Education: Issues and Perspectives*. New York: Wiley. Print.

Beinart, P. (2000). *The crisis of Zionism*. New York: Times Books, 2012. Print.

Beinart, Peter. (2012). *The Crisis of Zionism*. New York: Times/Henry Holt. Print.

Bernfeld, S. (1973). *Sisyphus or the limits of education*. Los Angeles: University of California. Print.

Brettler, M. Z. (2005). *How to read the Bible*. Philadelphia: Jewish Publication Society. Print.

Bright, J. (1960). *John Bright. A history of Israel*. London: S.C.M. Print.

Britzman, D. P. (2009). *The very thought of education: Psychoanalysis and the impossible professions*. Albany: State University of New York. Print.

Bruner, J. (1960). *The process of education*. Cambridge, MA: Harvard University Press. Print.

Bruner, J. (1999). *The culture of education*. Cambridge, MA: Harvard University Press, 1996. Print.

Buber, M. (1934). *I and Thou* (2nd ed). New York: Charles Scribner's Sons. 1958.

Buber, Martin. (1937). *I and Thou*. Translated by Walter Kaufmann. New York. Charles. Print.

Chazan, Barry. (1978). The Language of Jewish Education: Crisis and Hope in the Jewish School. New York. Hartmore House. Print.

Chazan, Barry (2015). "A Linguistic Analysis of the Role of Israel in American Jewish Schooling" in *The Journal of Jewish Education*. 81, 5, 85–92.

Cohen, S. M., & Eisen, A. (2000). *The Jew within: Self, family and community in America*. Indianapolis: Indiana University Press. Print.

Cole, M. (1996). *Cultural psychology: A once and future discipline*. Cambridge, MA: Belknap of Harvard University Press. Print.

Cremin, L. (1988). *American education: The metropolitan experience, 1876–1980*. New York: Harper and Row.

Daniels, R. (1990). *Coming to America: A history of immigration and ethnicity in American life*. New York: HarperCollins. Print.

Dewey, J. (1938). *Experience and education*. New York: Macmillan. Print.

Durkheim, É. (1956). *Education and sociology*. Glencoe: Free. Print.

Eriksen, T. H. (2002). *Ethnicity and nationalism*. London: Pluto. Print.

Erikson, E. (1950). *Childhood and society*. New York: W.W. Norton, 1950. Print.

Erikson, E. H. (1980). *Identity and the life cycle*. New York: Norton. Print.

Essrig, H. and Segal, A. (1966). *Israel Today*. New York: UAHC.

Frankl, V. (1959). *Man's search for meaning*. Boston: Beacon Books.

Freud, S. (1900). *The interpretation of dreams*. New York: Basic Books, 2010. Print.

Freud, Sigmund. (1962). *Civilization and Its Discontents*. New York: W.W. Norton. Print.

Friedman, L. (1999). *Identity's architect: A biography of Erik H. Erikson*. New York: Scribner's.

Friling, T., & Troen, I. S. (1998). Proclaiming Independence: Five Days in May from Ben-Gurion's Diary. *Israel Studies, 3*(1), 170–194.

Gazzaniga, M. S. (2005). *The ethical brain.* New York: Dana. Print.

Gopnik, A. (2009). *The philosophical baby: What children's minds tell us about truth, love, and the meaning of life.* New York: Farrar, Straus and Giroux. Print.

Graff, G. (2013). *And thou shalt teach them diligently to your children: A concise history of Jewish education in the United States 1776–2000.* New York: Jewish Theological Seminary. Print.

Hartman, D. (1978). *Joy and responsibility: Israel, modernity, and the renewal of Judaism.* Jerusalem: Ben-Zvi Posner. Print.

Hoffman, L. A. (1986). *The land of Israel: Jewish perspectives.* Notre Dame: University of Notre Dame. Print.

Holinger, David A. (1995). *Postethnic America: Beyond Multiculturalism.* New York. Basic. Print.

Hollinger, D. (2000). *Postethnic America: Beyond multiculturalism.* New York: Basic Books, 2016. Print.

Horowitz, B. (2012). Identity and beyond. N. pag. Web.

Jaeger, Werner (1943). *Paideia: The Ideals of Greek Culture.* New York: Oxford University Press. Print.

Korczak, J. (1919). *Loving every child.* Chapel Hill: Algonquin Books of Chapel Hill, 2007. Print.

Kugel, J. L. (2007). *How to read the Bible: A guide to scripture, then and now.* New York: Free. Print.

Magid, S. (2013). *American post-Judaism: Identity and renewal in a postethnic society.* Indianapolis: Indiana University Press. Print.

Noddings, Nel. (1992). *The Challenge to Care in Schools: An Alternative Approach to Education.* New York: Teachers College Press. Print.

Oakshott, M. (1989). *The voice of liberal learning: Michael Oakshott on education.* New Haven: Yale University Press. Print.

Palmer, P. J. (1998). *The courage to teach: Exploring the inner landscape of a teacher's life.* San Francisco: Jossey-Bass. Print.

Piaget, J. (1969). *Science of education and the psychology of the child.* New York: Penguin Books. Print.

Rogers, C. R. (1969). *Freedom to learn: A view of what education might become.* Columbus: C.E. Merrill Publishing. Print.

Rogers, C. (1980). *Freedom to learn.* New York: Merrill Publishing Company, 1986. Print.

Sarna, J. D. (2004). *American Judaism: A history.* New Haven: Yale University Press. Print.

Scheffler, I. (1950). *The Language of Education.* Springfield, Il. Charles C. Thomas.

Scheffler, I. (1960). *The language of education.* Springfield: Charles E. Thomas, 1950. Print.

Scheffler, I. (1991). *In praise of the cognitive emotions and other essays in the philosophy of education*. New York: Routledge. Print.

Soltis, J. (1978). *An introduction to the analysis of educational concepts*. Reading: Addison-Wesley. Print.

Vygotsky, L. S. (1978). *Mind in society. The development of higher psychological processes*. Cambridge, MA: Harvard University Press, 1980. Print.

Vygotsky, Lev (1994). *The Vygotsky Reader*. London. Wiley-Blackwell.

Wilson, J. Q. (1993). *The moral sense*. New York: Free. Print.

Woocher, J. and Woocher, M. (2013). "Jewish Education in a New Century: An Ecosystem in Transition" in *The American Jewish Yearbook*. New York: American Jewish Committee.

Woocher, J., & Woocher, M. (2014). Jewish education in a new century: An ecosystem in transition. In *American Jewish Yearbook 2013*. Springer, 2013. Print.

Wright, R. (1994). *The moral animal*. New York: Vintage. Print.

NOTES

1. The word "homeland" has distinct nuances and especially gender differences in various languages. In German and its variants, the word for homeland is the masculine Vaterland. Like German, Afrikaans uses the masculine Vaderland. The French phrase La Mere Patrie, the Russian word Rodina, the Hebrew word Moledet, and the Arabic Balad and Beledi are feminine.

2. The word "homeland" is not found in the "songbook" of foundational songs and anthems of America—*The Stars Spangled Banner*; *My Country Tis of Thee*; *America the Beautiful* or *This Land is Your Land This Land is My Land*.

3. All three provisions of the Homeland Act of 2002 link the term "homeland" with terrorism: (1) preventing terrorist attacks, (2) reducing vulnerability to terrorism, and (3) minimizing damage and assisting in recovery from terrorist attacks (Homeland Act 2012). This usage was reinforced by a television series of the same name produced by Showtime which follows the ongoing saga of agents and counter-agents preoccupied with radical religious terrorism in America and abroad.

4. Erikson notes that he first heard the term "identity" used by the Viennese psychoanalyst and member of the Freudian circle Paul Federn (Friedman, 1999). Freud used the word "identity" in his famous speech in 1926 to the B'nai B'rith Society in which he affirms his Jewishness. Ironically, Freud seems to use the term much as American Jews came to use it – linkage to a feeling of Jewishness.

5. Friedman indicates that Erikson himself may have helped this popularization with the publication (at his publisher's insistence) of the volume *Identity: Youth and Crisis* focusing on the concept of "identity crisis" and in which he used his terms somewhat loosely (Erikson 1980).

6. While there are many linguistic and homiletic attempts to explicate the meaning of the word, scholars remain uncertain about its exact meaning (Brettler 2005; Kugel 2007).
7. It is interesting to conjecture why Jews in the twentieth century chose this concept from contemporary psychology. One possibility is they sought the legitimacy and gravitas that came from adapting a concept created by a famous contemporary psychologist (Friedman 1999). A second possibility is that they were searching for an English term that did not have the sound of immigrant languages, such as the Yiddish word Yiddishkeit (a feeling of being Jewish) or the Hebrew word Halacha (strictly follow the 613 laws of Judaism). At the same time, they sought a term with enough ambiguity to signify affiliation but which in no way defined any specific criteria or demands; in "identity" they seemed to have found the perfect term.
8. Two noteworthy exceptions are an article by Bethamie Horowitz entitled "Jewish Identity and Beyond" (Horowitz 2012) and the book by Steven M. Cohen and Arnold Eisen *The Jew Within* (Cohen and Eisen 2000).
9. The field of Israel education has grown significantly in the past decade. There is a growing literature of academic articles, and studies written by academics, independent researchers, and foundations. A Reader's Guide on Israel Education was produced by the Berman Jewish Policy Archive at New York University. Two issues of the Journal of Jewish Education were devoted to the subject. Two books have been written on the subject in the past five years: *Israel Education Matters* by Lisa Grant and Ezra Kopelowitz, and *Loving the Real Israel: An Educational Guide for Liberal Zionism* by Alex Sinclair. A network of researchers of Jewish education has established Israel education as one of its research areas. The iCenter for Israel Education was established in 2008 in North America, and an Israel-based center for Israel education, Makom, was established in Israel in 2000.

2

Making Israel Education Happen

Abstract The subject of Israel education is not Israel but the fostering of a personal relationship with Israel. The contents of Israel education are narratives created over the ages that reflect an overall commitment to the Land of Israel as a core Jewish value. The meanings of these narratives changed over time, and there is no one core narrative. The special case of teaching contemporary Israel is discussed, and a new paradigm for teaching this topic is presented. The existence of non-Jewish narratives of Israel must also be presented within the context of Israel education.

Keywords Covenantal • Exilic Judaism • Virtue epistemology • *Havruta* • Jewish and non-Jewish narratives • Values education

Chapter 1 focused on principles of Israel education. Educators and teachers may nod their heads in agreement with these principles, but they legitimately have some practical questions. What are the specific aims of Israel education? What are the contents to be taught; and how do we teach these contents? In order to assist us in answering those questions in this chapter, we shall briefly focus on some key words used in the practice of education. Words make a difference, and how words about education are used significantly affects how education occurs.

The word "aim" in education refers to the purpose of an educational activity; it states the direction toward which education is oriented. It is the answer to the question "why are we doing what we are doing?" Aims are

© The Author(s) 2016

B. Chazan, *A Philosophy of Israel Education*,

DOI 10.1007/978-3-319-30779-4_2

an important link between some of the larger visions about life and education and more specific issues related to subject, contents, and pedagogies. The aims of Israel education, according to the relational approach, are to initiate a relationship between an individual and the Land of Israel and to make Israel a meaningful dimension of the individual's character.

The word "subject" is generally used in education to refer to spheres of knowledge that constitute a curriculum or course of study. These spheres of knowledge were once assumed to be reflective of mental faculties essential for a student's intellectual development (Pinar et al. 1999). The phrase a "subject-centered education" is often used to refer to approaches that focus on the transmission of worthwhile bodies of knowledge. We use the word "subject" differently; for us a subject is a person. We believe that education is first and foremost about the individual; it is about human bodies and not bodies of knowledge. Therefore, the subject of Israel education is not the Land of Israel, but, rather, a person's relationship with the Land of Israel. According to this conception of a "subject-centered" Israel, education is one that focuses on the learner.

The word "contents" typically refers to topics taught in schools. For example, the contents of history are often regarded as the investigation of past events, societies, and civilizations and the contents of science are described as the study of knowledge about natural systems and the understanding of the processes by which such knowledge is attained (Hazen and Trefil 2009; Wineburg 2001). The content of Israel education encompasses the investigative, but ultimately its focus is in the realm of values. While Israel education unquestionably includes historical and sociological dimensions, this in itself does not exhaust the content since Israel education is ultimately about values and character. The Land of Israel is a value that has shaped Jewish life in past and in present. Its importance is related to both collective Jewish experience and to personal life and meaning. For all these reasons, we categorize Israel education not as history education, ethnic education, or religious education, but rather as values education.

The word "pedagogy" refers to methodologies and practices used in the daily work of the educator. Pedagogies are activities used in formal and informal educational settings to educate the young. There is no one fixed pedagogy for all education. Specific pedagogies emerge from distinct contents. Moreover, diverse cultures create their own distinctive pedagogies, which are shaped by ideals, values, and customs. In that sense, pedagogies are not neutral, but rather reflect viewpoints about the meaning of education, society, and knowledge.

Texts and Narratives as Contents

The content of Israel education is the value of the Land of Israel.[1] As we have noted, this value has been important to Jewish civilization and has personal meaning for many Jews in the past and present. At the same time, there have been a variety of meanings of "The Land Israel" over time, and there is not one conclusive definition (Hoffman 1986; Segal 1987). These varied meanings are contained in a rich collection of diverse primary texts which constitute content of Israel education.

For pedagogues of Israel education, this vast collection of texts is formidable and requires some apparatus to make it accessible. The contemporary educator needs a reliable, conceptual GPS or framing structure in order to navigate this large landscape of education. Jewish education is fortunate to be able to draw upon the work of academicians who have devoted great energy to explicating the philosophy, history, sociology, and literature related to the Land of Israel. These academicians are the content specialists or experts who contribute to our understanding of the various meanings and who are helpful in developing diverse conceptual categories for organizing these narratives. Let us look at one model of categories of the meanings of the Land of Israel (Hoffman 1986; Lopatin 2015; Segal 2005).

The *covenantal* narrative refers to the biblical idea of the Land of Israel as the sign of a covenant between an omnipotent and omniscient deity who is the controlling force in history and in the lives of the people of Israel. This covenant calls upon the Israelites to follow the Godly will as enunciated in the Torah, and in return they will be God's People. The Land of Israel constitutes the official seal of this covenant:

And the Lord said to Abram "Go forth from your native land and from your father's house to the land that I shall show you
   I will make of you a great nation
   And I will bless you". (*Genesis:* 12:1–2)
   And the Lord said to Abram "raise up your eyes and look from where you are. Raise up your eyes to the north and south, to the east and the west, for I give you all that land that you see to you and your offspring forever". (*Genesis:* 13:14)
   I will maintain my covenant between me and you and your offspring to come as an everlasting covenant throughout the ages to be God to you and to your offspring to come... I assign the land you sojourn in to you and your offspring to come all the land of Canaan as an everlasting holding. (*Genesis:*17:7–8)

The *spiritual* narrative refers to the idea of Israel as both the historic birthplace of the Jewish people and as an ongoing symbol of important religious and moral ideas and practices. It reflects the effort of post-biblical rabbis to transform a Jerusalem-cultic-centered religion into an exilic Judaism which preserves the concept of the Land of Israel but makes it relevant and communicative to the lives of Jews now living in many places throughout the world.

> Jerusalem
> The words have gone out of the land and entered holy books.
> She is the city where waiting for God was born ...
> This is a city never indifferent to the sky ... Prayers are vibrant
> The Sabbath finds it hard to go away
> Jerusalem is a witness, an echo of eternity. (Heschel 1983, 14–116)

The *emancipatory* narrative emerges from the Jewish confrontation with modernity and the shift in focus from a worldview rooted in an omniscient and omnipotent deity who controls history, to a worldview which regards history as shaped by human beings and reason. Modernity also encompassed a re-organization of social structures, making the state the paramount social framework and source of power. Many Jews who adopted modern viewpoints wrestled with the possibility of becoming fully integrated members of modern societies, while still retaining some form of link with their past and their people (Mendes-Flohr and Reinharz 1980). This search led to several alternative solutions, such as conversion, assimilation, reform, ultra-orthodoxy, Bundism, socialism, Jewish culturalism, and Zionism:

> The National Assembly, conceding that the requisite to be a French citizen, and to become an active citizen, are fixed by the constitution, and every man who, being duly qualifies, takes the civic oath, and engages to fulfill all the duties prescribed by the constitution, has right to all the advantages it assures, annuals all adjournment, restrictions, no exceptions, contained in the preceding decrees, affecting individuals of the Jewish persuasion, who shall take the civic oath, which shall be considered as a renunciation of all privileges in their favor. (French National Assembly, Emancipation of the Jews France, September 28, 1791)

The *Zionist* narrative was one of several narratives to emerge from the Jewish confrontation with modernity. It reflected one solution to the desire to be a nation like all other people, while retaining distinctive Jewish elements. When some Jews lost faith in the possibility of attaining the goal of integration into societies, they came to regard the idea of a Jewish homeland as the only viable solution to "the Jewish problem". Therefore, they claimed that Jews needed to live in their own land where they could be both human and Jewish:

> Nothing prevents us from being and remaining exponents of a united humanity, when we have country of our own. To fulfill this mission we do not have to remain literally planted among the nations who hate us and despise us let sovereignty be granted us over a portion of the earth's surface large enough to satisfy our rightful requirements as a nation. The rest we shall manage ourselves. (Herzl Diaries 1956)

The *Jewish state* narrative conceives of Israel as a modern state where Jews can live freely as Jews (or Israelis) and as human beings. This narrative retains links to the Jewish past and to the world of Jewry in the present. It regards Israel as nation like all other nations, while also having unique Jewish characteristics:

> *Eretz Yisrael* was the birthplace of the Jewish people. Here their spiritual religious and political identity was shaped. Here they first attained statehood, created cultural values of nations and universal significance and gave to the world the eternal book of books.
> On the 29th of November 1947 the United Nations General Assembly passed a resolution calling for the establishment of a Jewish State in *Eretz Yisrael* ... This recognition by the United Nations of the right of the Jewish people to establish their State is irrevocable. This right is the natural right of the Jewish people to be master of their own fate, like all other nations, in their own sovereign State, the State of Israel will be based on freedom, justice, and peace as envisaged by the prophets of Israel. It will ensure complete equality of social and political rights to all its inhabitants. It will guarantee freedom of religion, education and culture. (*Megilat Ha'atzma'ut The Declaration of Independence of the State of Israel*, May 1948)

The *peoplehood* narrative says that Jewishness refers to an historical and contemporary civilization which enconpasses culture, values, customs, a language, and a land which is a source of pride and connection to Jews around the world. This narrative conceives of Judaism as an all-encompassing civilization which includes religion, religious law, customs and mores, language, culture, and a state.[2]

Judaism is far more comprehensive than Jewish religion. It includes that nexus of a history, literature, language, social organization, folk sanctions, standards of conduct, social and spiritual ideals, and esthetic values, which in their totality form a civilization. (Kaplan, 178)

Judaism cannot maintain continuity without an environment where it will be able to exercise a civilization's primary prerogative. Palestine is the only land which can furnish such an environment for Jewish civilization. (Kaplan, 273)

Judaism as an entity is unlikely to survive either as an ancillary or co-coordinate civilization unless it thrives as a primary civilization in Palestine. (Kaplan, 273)

There are multiple texts which reflect these various narratives. Moreover, the ordering of these narratives is not exclusively chronological. Indeed, contemporary Israeli society may be regarded as an arena in which these various narratives continue to interact and conflict with each other on a daily basis. In that sense, these narratives are not just historical documents, but they also are living stories.

PEDAGOGIES

The discussion of pedagogies flows directly from the analysis of aims and contents. A relational pedagogy of Israel education focuses on reading, analyzing, and discussing diverse texts and asking questions and discussing answers. The essence of this methodology is a pedagogy of relating and relationships (Lanski et al. 2015). The educator has multiple roles in this process. The first task is to choose "texts that talk", that is, sources that are accessible to the young at various ages. The next step is to read, analyze, and dissect sources together with the students so as to first understand words and then to explore meanings and ideas. Then the educator's role is to create personal interaction between students and text, students and students, and texts and texts. This process can include enabling students to, as it were, meet and talk with interesting figures from the Jewish past and present. The young should have the opportunity to sit in Abraham and Sarah's tent near Beer Sheva, meet with Dr. Theodor Herzl in Café Central in Vienna, have coffee with Golda Meir at Caffit in Jerusalem, and meet with Mordecai Kaplan in Starbucks in New York. The questions for discussion in these meetings might include: "Abraham, what does the word covenant mean?"; "What were the boundaries of the Land God promised to you?"; "Dr. Herzl you are not religious. Why do you want a Jewish State?"; "Mrs. Meir, why did you change your name from Myerson to Meir?"; "Dr. Kaplan, why do you say that Judaism is not a religion?"[3] The teacher's role throughout the process is not to give the right answer, but rather to sustain a process of questions and answers. Sometimes, teachers also have a responsibility for correcting what might be called "glaring mistakes", such as focusing on Genesis as a chronology of Jewish history and neglecting the central purpose of these texts as the presentation of "big ideas" about the deity, humanity, history, and land.[3] It is important for educators to engage in a summative activity which provides some shape to the flow of the entire process and minimizes the sense that "it was fun but all we did was talk".

There is a rich library of Jewish texts, which reflect the diverse views on the meaning of the Land of Israel.[4] The texts of the biblical, talmudic and rabbinic eras are ideal primary sources for this approach. The prayer book contains many references to the Land of Israel, and it has the advantage of being a book that the young are likely to encounter in their pre-adolescent years. Zionist literature is replete with stories, memoirs, ideological treatises, and fiction advocating its cause. Contemporary Israel is the ultimate treasure chest of sources: street sounds, muezzin voices, church bells, a siren in Jerusalem announcing the imminent beginning of the Sabbath. Israel is street graffiti, political debates, pop and hip-hop music, art, dance, foods, and, most importantly, people. The doorway to these contemporary Israel education resources is increasingly available via the ubiquitous cell phones, iPad, and smart watches which currently are the ultimate pedagogical tools.

There are several pedagogic approaches from general and Jewish cultures which have much to offer in terms of reading and analyzing textual narratives. Such approaches encourage analysis beyond the literal word in order to find meanings that are either implicit in the text or that the student hears.[5] The interpretive process can motivate learners to talk with texts, and to query them about their meanings beyond the literal. The American curriculum theorist William Pinar suggests that the traditional Jewish methodologies of analysis of biblical and rabbinic texts have important potential for the reconceptualization of contemporary American curriculum:

> I point to the two intellectually "repressed" traditions in the field, specifically Jewish and international studies, whose articulation now restructure the reconceptualization of curriculum studies in the United States. (Pinar, 73)

The implication of the interpretive process of traditional Jewish texts has been discussed by a group of contemporary Jewish educators who describe a variety of educational orientations to teaching biblical and rabbinic texts. These diverse orientations include the historical, the moralistic, the personal, the ideational, the action-oriented, and the commandment-oriented texts.[6] Since so many of the classical texts deal with the meaning of the Land of Israel, the literature of teaching biblical and rabbinic texts is a valuable resource for Israel educators.

Questioning is an important educational methodology with roots in classical non-Jewish and Jewish traditions (Dimitrovsky 1980; Marrou 1956; Jaeger 1986, 42). Socrates, Odysseus, Rabbi Akiva, and St. Augustine are but a few champions of the value of the question.[7] These traditions emphasized the virtues of a beautiful question as much as of the right answer.[8] The contemporary focus on the question is central to contemporary business, innovation, and entrepreneurship, which declare that the challenges of modern life are as much related to the ability to ask big questions as they are to dispensing a quick-fix solutions (Drew and Jacobberg 2014; Berger 2014). Questions about the Land of Israel are not a problem for Israel education, but are, rather, an important window of opportunity for discussion about a value that matters.

Collaborative learning is an approach that focuses on students working together, listening to each other, sharing viewpoints, and learning how to utilize diverse skill sets in the discussion of issues. Through working together, students are able to realize that learning is both an individual and a group process. Some Jewish educationists connect the concept of collaborative learning with a classical approach called *havruta*[9]:

> *Havruta* means companionship or friendship. It is an extension of the Hebrew word "*haver*", companion or friend. In its common use the word *havruta* can refer to the learning pair, and/or to the practice of paired learning itself. In using the term "*havruta* text study" we mean to refer to the symbiotic relationship between a text and two *havruta* learning partners. (Holzer and Kent, 1)

This technique expresses the belief that learning is not a lonely act of the individual but, rather, a collective and communal experience.

> Just as in the case of iron when one implement sharpens the other, so too do two Torah scholars sharpen each other.... just as fire cannot be made to

burn with one piece of wood alone so the words of Torah cannot be retained by one who studies alone. (Holzer and Kent, 6)

Value education and pedagogy has been a long-standing and central dimension of the world of educational thinking (Chazan 1985). In the second half of the last century, American psychologist and educator Lawrence Kohlberg proposed an approach to moral education rooted in a six-stage model of cognitive moral development.[10] While Kohlberg's psychological theory of moral development became a much debated and questioned topic, his pedagogy of moral education has had widespread use. This approach, called dilemma discussion, encompasses the following: (1) reading together a short description of a specific moral dilemma, (2) asking someone to briefly summarize the story to be sure that there is agreement about to the facts, (3) asking "What should x (the protagonist in the story) do and why? (4) conducting a group discussion in which students discuss various choices and their reasons, and (5) summarizing the discussion without defining any specific answer as the right one. This technique highlights the role of reasoning about issues of values and creates a safe environment for open value discussion. It is an accessible and useful framework for navigating the many diverse landscapes of Israel narratives.

Virtue epistemology and pedagogy is a field in contemporary philosophy, which argues (as did Scheffler) that value decisions are neither inherently affective or capricious, but, rather, are characterized by "intellectual character virtues" or "faculty virtues" such as conscientiousness, open-mindedness, attentiveness, intellectual tenacity, the desire to know, and courage.[11] We decide to choose what we value in some reflective way, which, at the same time, is fueled by much affect and passion. In that sense, value education is about both thinking and reflecting and about feeling and identifying. This approach implies that study of the value of the Land of Israel should be implemented in a manner that is passionately deliberative and courageously open. It is driven by the desire to understand something that matters. This discussion is not a triumphal testimony for a preordained ideology, but rather an engaging activity of mind and the heart. It is a pedagogy of relationship, reason, and resonance.

The Russian psychologist Lev Vygotsky's notion of the zone of proximal development adds an important developmental element to our discussion of pedagogies (Vygotsky 1999). While observing children's learning, Vygotsky noticed that there was one type of learning, namely, language, which children could do more or less independently or spontaneously as part of the normal process of development. In contrast, there were skills, which were too difficult for children to master on their own. In between these two poles, there is an area, which he called the zone of proximate development, in which children can master certain skills with guidance and encouragement from a knowledgeable person, teacher, or group. In terms of Israel, this means there are topics that may require minimal "teaching" interventions, while there are other topics which call for a much greater proactive role of teacher and the classroom community. This developmental approach means that contents and methodologies must speak to the child's specific zone of proximal development. The voices of Vygotsky, Piaget, Korczak, and Bruner continue to remind us to never underestimate the child.

When discussing the practice of Israel education, it is important to realize that there is the temptation to co-opt methodologies which may seem attractive because they are contemporary or stylish, and then arbitrarily impose them on Israel education. At the same time, there is much to learn from general education and traditional Jewish education that is relevant for pedagogy of Israel education. Nevertheless, methodologies are not "one-size-fits-all" garments. Rather, they are finely woven, tailor-made garments specific to the body and being of each person. In that sense, the act of education and being educated is a very personal work of art.

THE ISSUE OF CONTEMPORARY STATE OF ISRAEL

Teaching about contemporary Israel deserves special attention since this is both a topic with few precedents in Jewish or general education, as well as a highly charged subject. The newness of the topic, combined with its emotional dimensions, has often rendered the practice of teaching contemporary Israel either ambiguous or provoking.[12] The ambiguity flows from the difficulty of framing its content. Purely historical frames frequently underestimate the contemporary state. Purely spiritual frames generally choose to emphasize Heavenly Jerusalem and to disregard earthly Tel Aviv. Geo-political and sociological approaches often focus on politics, problems, and conflict, and neglect social, cultural, and spiritual dynamics.

A mode that became popular in twentieth-century Jewish education is what might be called "the Americanization of Israel" frame. It is best exemplified in Otto Preminger's 1960 film version of Leon Uris' book *Exodus*.[13] Preminger's Israel was the saga of Israel as a modern American democracy, which transformed the desert into blooming fields, was led by handsome hardened and committed heroes and heroines, and was forced to defend itself against indigenous populations who opposed the new state. Teaching Israel was not able to evolve a frame that emphasized the new but did not neglect the old, and that was honest and real but that was also inspiring and engaging.

The relational approach attempts to develop a new paradigm for presenting contemporary Israel rooted in four points of reference: (1) the role of home and homeland in human life, (2) the mindsets of contemporary young people, (3) the importance of Israel to the Jewish people, and (4) a multi-dimensional picture of the dynamics of the twenty-first-century state. These reference points are chosen because they present Israel in the broader context of the modern world and relate to ways of thinking of the twenty-first-century youth. This framing is translated into five 'lenses':

Lens 1 The modern State of Israel is an improbable and unlikely phenomenon. It is what Nassim Nicholas Taleb described as a "black swan event" which is an occurrence that (1) lies outside the realm of normal expectations, (2) carries extreme impact, and (3) after the fact, there is a pronounced effort to make it seem obvious and predictable (Taleb 2007). For almost 2000 years, the majority of the Jewish people did not live in the Land of Israel. In 1948, a modern Jewish state was established which today is home to almost half of world Jewry. This is an out-of-the-ordinary event for the Jewish people and for the world. As Taleb indicated, there are numerous historical and political analyses that were developed to prove that this was obvious all along. They may be right and they may be wrong, but the fact is that this new state is some kind of statement about the role of the improbable in the flow of personal life and social history.

Lens 2 The State of Israel was created by a variety of Jewish ideologies that came together for a brief moment to agree on one thing—the creation of a Jewish state. Since that state was created, the story of its existence has been greatly shaped by the ongoing interactions of these diverse ideologies. All the issues of statehood, including education, religion and state, culture, democracy, and theocracy, are hammered out within the context of this variegated ideological environment. Sometimes, these interactions have been creative and fruitful; usually, they have been characterized by friction, and, sadly, there have been times that they have been tragic. The saga of these interactions is an important lens for understanding and relating to contemporary Israel.

Lens 3 The State of Israel does not exist in a vacuum. It is located in a part of the world that is a meeting place of people from diverse national, cultural, and religious sectarian backgrounds and sometimes violent ideologies. It is a state closely identified with Western nations and political cultures. Its dynamics are shaped as much by international politics as they are by internal Israeli politics. The dynamics of the contemporary State of Israel, like Jewish life throughout history, is not outside of general history, but in many ways because of it. One cannot look at contemporary Israel with Jewish eyes only; rather, the multiple lenses of the world civilization in which we live, and particularly the current clash of civilizations, is an indispensable lens in the camera toolkit.

Lens 4 For most of its history, the Jewish people were small groups existing in larger societies. As such, they were "the other" both because of their size and because of their commitment to the preservation of a particular identity. The Jewish people were also relatively powerless in terms of socio-economic, military, or demographic forces. Any power the Jewish people had was its spiritual capital. The creation of the State of Israel changed these dynamics. Today Israel is the "we" and its non-Jewish minorities are the "other". This situation became even more complicated because of the ongoing geo-political conflict to which we referred. The realities that the new state faced resulted in new challenges of majority–minority and "us" and "them" for a people not used to being a majority and not used to having power.

Lens 5 The State of Israel is home to approximately seven million Jews. It is also important to the millions of other Jews who live elsewhere but who share a deep sense of connection to the survival, achievements, and people of the contemporary state. The State of Israel and world Jewry have developed ties of mutual responsibility. The lens of looking at contemporary Israel must focus both within and also at the interaction with world Jewry.

These frames—the unprecedented, multiple narratives, the Jewish and the general, the other and power, and Israel and world Jewry—shape the pedagogy of teaching contemporary Israel. This pedagogy encompasses a broad box of lenses, which includes the political, the economic, the social, the ideological, the cultural, as well as those moments in Israeli daily life when babies are born, elderly pass away, love is found, and love is lost.

Some people fear such diverse sets of lenses lest it reveal the good, the bad, and the ugly. However, a panoramic view, which includes some fuzzy black and white snapshots, need not destroy this engaging and out-of-the ordinary saga. Societies have many faces, and the many faces of Israel present a diverse, rich, dynamic modern society with links to the past and to Jews worldwide. All of the photographs are not pretty, and like all photographs what one sees depends on where one was standing when taking the picture. The presentation of a multi-dimensional, multi-lensed portrait is likely to tell a story worth telling and worth becoming part of one's own family album.

The discussion of teaching contemporary Israel would not be complete without dealing with the existence of significant non-Jewish religious, ethnic, and political narratives of the land of Israel. These narratives are long-standing value statements that must be understood and cannot be dismissed because they are the "other". Israel education should not approach this task with the intent to dehumanize or demonize non-Jewish narratives simply because they are "the other". In the process of learning and becoming comfortable with their own narrative, Jews must understand the contents of the other narratives and where they differ. Therefore, Israel education should deal with these narratives by looking at core documents, historical, geographical, and ideological dimensions, and current manifestations of them in practice. Jewish educators can legitimately claim that their mission is to educate young Jews and to generate a relationship with the place called Israel. This need not be at the expense of neglect of the other narratives. The passion to affirm one's own narrative should encompass the courage to understand divergent views.

We have had a long journey in a few pages in this chapter—from aim to content to pedagogy. Our journey is not yet over. In the next chapter, we turn to the role of an immersive culture and the nature of the Israel educator in a relational philosophy of Israel education.

BIBLIOGRAPHY

Berger, W. (2014). *A more beautiful question: The power of inquiry to spark breakthrough ideas.* New York: Bloomsbury. Print.

Boyd, Drew and Jacob Goldenberg (2014). *Inside the Box: A Proven System for Breakthrough Results.* New York: Simon and Shuster. Print.

Chazan, Barry. (1985). *Contemporary Approaches to Moral Education: Analyzing Alternative Theories.* New York: Teachers College Press. Print.

Cummings, E. E. (1972). *Complete Poems, 1913–1962.* New York: Harcourt Brace Jovanovich. Print.

Dimitrovsky, Zalman (1976). *Exploring the Talmud: Volume 1*. Education. New York: Ktav house. Print.

Hazen, Robert and James Trefil. (2009). *Science Matters: Achieving Scientific Literacy*. New York: Anchor. Print.

Herzl, Theodor. (1956). The Diaries of Theodor Herzl. New York: Dial Press.

Heschel, Abraham Joshua and Samuel Dresner. (1983). I Asked for Wonder: ASpiritual Anthology. New York: Crossroad. Print.

Hoffman, L. A. (1986). *The land of Israel: Jewish perspectives*. Notre Dame: University of Notre Dame. Print.

Jaeger, Werner. (1986). *Paideia: The Ideals of Greek Culture*. New York: Oxford University Press. 2nd Edition. Print.

Kaplan, M. M. (2010). *Judaism as a civilization: Toward a reconstruction of American-Jewish life*. Philadelphia: Jewish Publication Society. Print.

Lanski, A., Stewart, A., & Werchow, Y. (2015). Relating and relationships. *The Aleph Bets of Israel education*. N. pag. www.theicenter.org. The iCenter for Israel Education. Web.

Lopatin, Asher (2015). "The Place of Israel in Jewish Tradition" N.pag. www. theicenter.org. The iCenter for Jewish education. Web.

Mendes-Flohr, P., & Reinharz, J. (Eds.). (1980). *The Jew in the modern world*. New York: Oxford University Press. Print.

Pinar, William et al (1995). *Understanding Curriculum: An Introduction to the Study of Historical and Contemporary Curriculum Discourse*. New York: P. Lang, 1995. Print.

Pinar et al. (1999). *Understanding curriculum: An introduction to the study of historical and contemporary curriculum discourses*. New York: P. Lang, 1995. Print.

Segal, B. J. (2005). *Returning: The Land of Israel as focus in Jewish history*. iUniverse. Inc.

Sosa, E. (1991). *Knowledge in perspective*. Cambridge, MA: Cambridge University Press. Print.

Taleb, N. N. (2007). *The Black Swan: The impact of the highly improbable*. New York: Random House. Print.

Weinburg, Sam (2001). *Historical Thinking and other Unusual Acts*. Philadelpha: Temple University Press. Print.

NOTES

1. Values are ideals or beliefs that one holds dear. They often refer to core principles, which guide our lives. Value education is one of the many terms often used synonymously or closely with each other, e.g., moral education, character education, and humanistic education. See Brad Art. *What is the Best: An Introduction to Ethics Belmont, CA*: Wadsworth Publishing Company, 1993) R. M. Here, *The Language of Morals* Oxford University Press, London: 1964).

2. Mordecai Kaplan was an American Jewish philosopher who contended that twentieth-century American Jewry was in need of a new conceptual frame, which he called Jewish civilization. His magnum opus on this subject was *Judaism as a Civilization*, New York: Jewish Publication Society 1934.

3. It is important to allow a free flow of discussion, but teachers also have the responsibility of correcting errors that would otherwise hamper fruitful discussion. One of the glaring mistakes is teaching Torah as history rather than as a major treatise about the nature of being human, ethics and morals, the meaning of a deity, order and chaos. See: Marc Brettler. *How to Read the Bible* (Philadelphia: Jewish Publication Society, 2005), and James Kugel: *How to Read the Bible: A Guide to Scripture Then and Now* (New York: Free Press, 2007).

4. At the beginning of the twentieth century, the poet Chaim Nacman Bialik and his colleague Yehoshua Hana Ravnitzky created an extensive compendium of rabbinic legends from the Talmudic Midrash literature. The book was originally published in Hebrew in Odessa between 1918 and 1922. It was subsequently reprinted in many editions in Palestine. They called their book *Sefer Ha Aggadah* which while translated as the "Book of Legends" was actually a remarkable collection of homiletic literature from the Talmudic and rabbinic world. There are several sections that deal with selections about the meaning of the Land of Israel. Rabbi William Braudes translated the book into English in 1992. *The book of Legends: Sefer Ha Aggadah Legends from the Talmud and Midrash* (New York: Schocken Books, 1992). It is a useful resource for sources from classical texts about the meaning of Israel.

5. There is a theory that emphasizes the orality of ancient Jewish tradition. According to this approach, the Jews are better described as "people of the word", rather than "people of the book": (i) in Hebrew, the Ten Commandments are not commandments but rather words or statements, (ii) the *Shema* prayer calls upon the people to hear and listen; (iii) Jewish tradition speaks of two Torahs given on Sinai: the written Torah and the oral Torah of the rabbis. Moshe Idel refers to the Jews as "a sonorous or sound community", and Rabbi Ashkenazi stated that the Jews "are not the people of the book ... God did not chose a people of readers or libraries" (Handelman. *Make Yourself a Teacher*. Seattle: University of Washington Press, 2011). See also Amos Oz and Fania Oz-Salzberger *Jews and Words* (New Haven: Yale University Press, 2012).

6. The volume *Turn It and Turn it Again: Studies in the Teaching Learning of Classical Jewish Texts,* which focuses on teaching and learning classical texts, is a useful guide for the analysis of traditional texts. (Jon Levisohn and Susan Fendrick *Turn It Over and Turn It Over Again*. Brighton, MA: Academic Studies Press, 2013). See also Sophie Haroutunian-Gordon *Interpretive Discussion* (Cambridge, MA. Harvard University Press, 2014).

7. *Six Questions of Socrates* and *Teaching Plato in Palestine: Philosophy in a Divided World* are interesting studies of questioning in contemporary educational settings. (Christopher Phillips. *Six Questions of Socrates; A Modern-day Journey Through World Philosophy* (New York: W.W. Norton & Company, 2004; Carlos Frankl. *Teaching Plato in Palestine: Philosophy in a Divided World* Princeton: Princeton University Press, 2015).

8. The poet E.E. Cummings bemoaned the obsessive emphasis on the beautiful answer and the disregard of the beautiful question: "always the beautiful answer; who asks [about] a more beautiful question?" (Cummings 1972).

9. Holzer and Kent provide a comprehensive analysis of the traditional and contemporary philosophic underpinnings of *havruta* with references to rabbinic texts and to the writings of Hans-Georg Gadamer and Paul Ricoeur. The volume includes detailed pedagogy of texts, frameworks, questions, and evaluative tools of *havruta* study (Elie Holzer and Orit Kent, *A Philosophy of Havruta: Understanding and Teaching the Art of Text Study* (Boston, Ma: Academic Studies Press, 2013).

10. Lawrence Kohlberg was a psychologist who studied at the University of Chicago and subsequently established the Center for Moral Education at the Harvard Graduate School of Education. He trained a generation of scholars in the theory and practice of moral education and conducted research in schools, prisons, and other settings. Works by or about Kohlberg include Lawrence Kohlberg. *A Philosophy Moral Development. San Francisco: Harper and Row, 1981* and Brenda Munsey, editor. *Moral Development, Moral Education, and Kohlberg* Birmingham: Religious Education Press, 1980. Kohlberg and his colleagues created several summer seminars on moral development in Jewish education and published numerous articles. Many programs in the Jewish educational world were influenced by Kohlberg's approach.

11. Virtue epistemology is a collection of contemporary approaches in analytic philosophy of education that assigns an important role to what it calls "intellectual virtue concepts" in value discussions. Virtue epistemology comes to restore the role of intellectual responsibility in the value domain. See: Ernest Sosa. 1991. *Knowledge in Perspective*. Cambridge: Cambridge University Press, 1991 and Linda Zagzebski. (Cambridge, 1996). Dow's book *Virtuous Minds: Intellectual Character Development: For Students, Educators, Parents* is an interesting application of virtue ethics to faith-based school settings. Philip B. Dow: *Virtuous Minds: Intellectual Character Development: For Students, Educators, and Parents* (Downdraft, IL: Inter Varsity Press, 2013).

12. Several books and articles written in the last two decades discuss the complications of Israel education and propose new directions. See: Lisa Grant and Ezra Kopelowitz. *Israel Masters: a 21st Century Paradigm for Jewish*

Education (Jerusalem: Center for Jewish Peoplehood Education, 2012; Alec Sinclair). *The Aleph Bet of Israel Education, 2nd Edition* (Northbrook, The Center for Israel Education, 2015).

13. Leon Uris' novel was published in 1958 and Otto Preminger's film version in 1960. The novel and the subsequent film proved to be remarkable commercial successes. *Exodus* had great impact on the nascent Russian Jewish activist movement, whose founders circulated samizdat copies of the text, which ignited great excitement. A leader of the American Soviet Jewry Movement suggested that it was "probably more meaningful than even the Bible". M.M. Silver. *Leon Uris and Exodus: The Americanization of Israel's Founding Story* (Detroit: Wayne State University Press, 2010). In 2001, the influential Arabist thinker Edward Said commented that the novel constituted "the main narrative that dominates American thinking about the creation of Israel". *Al Ahram Weekly*, August 30–September 5, 2001.

3

A Culture of Israel Education

Abstract Israel education is rooted in a cultural approach, which focuses on the role of social contexts and dynamics in education. Immersive environments are settings, which can influence attitudes by virtue of their synergistic nature. Connectedness refers to social linkages created by social networks. Virtual communities offer opportunities for enhancing an immersive approach to Israel education. The Israel experience is a significantly new Jewish educational framework. As in all education, the educator is a seminal force in the realization of the educational vision.

Keywords Connectedness • Immersive • *Oeuvres* • Virtual communities • The Israel experience

The relational approach to Israel education is rooted in two educational perspectives, sometimes regarded as contradictory, but which we regard as complementary—the humanist and the culturalist. The humanist approach teaches us that the person is the focus of education, and the culturalist approach teaches us that cultures are shaping forces of who we are and what we might become. A synergistic view of these two perspectives suggests an all-encompassing Israel education which is nourished by a culture, while, at the same time, focused on the person. Relational Israel education combines the learned-centered approach and the culturalist approach to create a holistic educational practice. Chapter 2 emphasized the interaction of the young with texts, narratives, and ideas related to Israel, then

© The Author(s) 2016
B. Chazan, *A Philosophy of Israel Education*,
DOI 10.1007/978-3-319-30779-4_3

and now. This chapter focuses on the creation of a socio-cultural framework for Israel education. We examine several ideas about culture and context as threads which when woven together form the tapestry that we call "a culture of Israel education".

Immersive Environments

Consider how children ordinarily learn the ideas and values that are most cherished by their parents and their communities. Such learning takes place over time. It is not achieved through a specific course of instruction and is not affected in any one venue. It occurs through interaction with significant others who embody and are committed to such values. It is advanced through formative experiences that enable young people to actually participate in these ideas and values in their own lives. Being part of a community which shares these ideas and values is a unique experience. It is realized through opportunities to interact with peers and in order to better understand ideas, values, and behaviors.

Historically, this type learning occurred in families, local communities, and places of worship which together constituted holistic learning communities (Goitein 1999). These institutions were immersive environments where learning was advanced through conversation, practice, ritual, and relationships. The contemporary educational institutions that have come close to having such characteristics and achieving such outcomes are what sociologist Erving Goffman called "total institutions" (Goffman 1960). These are settings, such as boarding schools, army cadet programs, summer camps, or long-term retreats which can co-opt the full range of experiences in a day, a week, and a month to "speak" the language of the desired ideas and values. The chief characteristics of "total institutions" include the following: (1) all aspects of life are conducted in a similar place and under the same authority, (2) each phase of a member's life is carried out in the company of others, (3) all phases of the day's activities are tightly scheduled and sequenced, and (4) various activities are brought together in a single plan aimed at fulfilling the goals of the institution. For Goffman, the paradigmatic examples of total institutions were (ironically) prisons, convents, and mental hospitals, places that obviously don't offer the most desirable template for Israel education. At the same time, the notion of an immersive institution has much relevance for Israel education, and it is no coincidence that over the past 25 years, immersive educational frameworks of summer camps, retreats, educational travel programs, and the Israel experience have provided the Jewish community with the great hope for increased vitality (Soberman and Stewart 2015). These institutions are total or partial immersive environments where learning is advanced through setting, personnel, facilities, conversation, practice, ritual, and relationships, and they seem to have demonstrated a record of success. To be clear, the educational power of these programs derives not only from the amount of time, but more significantly from their immersiveness, from their capacity to submerge young people in a "total" experience. It suggests that, if we are to do better at achieving the multi-dimensional outcomes of Israel education, we need to more effectively utilize the full immersive capacity of our educational institutions.

In that sense, it can be said that Israel education should live in a broad totality of frameworks. It needs to totally permeate the lives of educational institutions: in mission statements, the consciousness of lay and professional leaders, formal and informal curricula, walls, halls, buses, music, holidays, and foods. Goffman believed that the non-verbal, non-cognitive, non-discursive elements of a culture are as important, or more so, for conveying cultural norms as the written word or the "classroom lesson." Numerous studies of unique school and other educational institutions across time and place echo this point[1] (Bettelheim 1950; A.S. Neill 1970; Redl and Wineman 1957; Peshkin 1986).

There is a notion often indigenous to schooling that there are core contents and "subjects" which constitute "curriculum", and there are clubs, sports, hobbies, arts, and culture which are "extracurricular" or secondary activities that enrich and embellish. In fact, the reality may be just the opposite. Indeed, in Israel education, it is these "extras" that very often are the educational essence. Sometimes a song, a story, a person, a fable, a recipe, or a picture connected to Israel touches those thousands of neurons in the mind, which lead to feeling, thinking, and doing. The immersive approach to Israel education argues that the distinction between "extra" and "core" is not compelling, since people learn and are affected in diverse ways. Don't regard the fluff as extra trim; for some, it may be the entryway into the heart of the matter. Essentially, what is being suggested is that educators must learn to "think immersively". Thinking immersively involves a sophisticated approach to education, which calls upon educators to co-opt a totality of senses, foci, and resources. Educators need to be cognizant of the conditions that constitute the given framework (ideological or denominational affiliation, size of institution, architecture of the institution, staff), and they should co-opt them to highlight and upgrade the Israel immersion of the institution. The ideal situation occurs when all the components of an immersion experience integrate, but that doesn't always happen. Too often, educators are forced to become harried hosts of a smorgasbord that becomes messy and non-aesthetic. The challenge of immersive education is to turn the buffet of diverse foods into an aesthetic dining experience in which the various components enhance each other.

It might be argued that this is a manipulative picture for Israel education. It might, but it need not be. It certainly is true that techniques of immersiveness have been used for indoctrination, but there also are many instances when they are employed as educative forces. The key is to retain the core vision—the relationship with Israel—in mind. One might also argue that given the realities of contemporary Jewish life, this immersive idea is simply too difficult to implement. Indeed, contemporary realities of Jewish life would seem to argue just the opposite; that is, these immersive activities are reported as life changing rather than the normal non-immersive structure of Jewish education.

CONNECTEDNESS

In their book entitled *Connected: the Surprising Power of Our Social Networks and How They Shape Our Lives*, Nicholas Christakis and James Fowler explore the science of social networks and its role in shaping lives. They combine traditions of social psychology and sociology with the new fields of neurosciences, genetic studies, and cyberspace to explore the role of networks, links, and paths in explaining the ways we learn and grow (Christakis and Fowler 2009). Christakis and Fowler suggest that (1) people are "connected" creatures, (2) there is a phenomenon (which they call a "contagion") of the spread and flow of information and attitudes flowing across network lines, (3) there is "a homophilic predisposition" to link with people who resemble us or whom we think we would like to be, and (4) networks can develop frameworks that attain lives of their own. Christakis and Fowler indicate that one of the ways we understand who we are is by experiencing ourselves in the mirror of people with whom we connect. These links have many degrees of separation, and ultimately our networks transcend our immediate contacts. A network community is a framework that can shape people and personality.

The notion of connectedness is not new to Jewish civilization. As a minority group living among larger groupings, Jews were invested in creating local and trans-geographical links with fellow Jews. This point is implied in popular interpretations of the talmudic phrase "every Israelite is responsible one for the other" (Babylonian Talmud; 39a) as meaning that there is a link and mutual responsibility between Jews over time and place. If one of the ways people learn how to be happy is by associating with happy people, one of the ways young Jews might be more Israel-connected is if they were to be in social networks of positively Israel-connected peers. The scaffolding of this Israel-connected process over the years of child's life (family albums, Skype, family trips, youth trips, learning Hebrew, youth retreats) is a worthy investment, whose outcomes will take time, but which is attainable and verifiable.

Virtual Communities

An important exemplar of contemporary connectedness is the "virtual community"—a group of people sharing common interests, ideas, and feelings over the Internet, which is made possible by the cyberspace revolution (Thomas and Brown 2011). The world of children, youth, young adults, and all people has dramatically expanded today to encompass virtual communities or digital networks. In a study of social media participation by youth and young adults, Mizuko Eto and colleagues researched the significance of the new technology for peer groupings, resulting in the creation of a tripartite typology of participation in social media (Eto 2011). The first level is called "hanging out"—becoming familiar with being with others in spaces mediated by digital technology. This level is not simply technical, but also social, and involves the process of building social identity. The second level is "messing around" which encompasses finding out more about, and experimenting with, one's personal identity on social media. This level is about beginning to explore topics of personal interest and discover them in a self-driven way. The third level is "geeking out" which means total comfort in using media in intense, autonomous, and interest-driven ways. It is a sense of embodiment and comfort in esoteric knowledge and personal interests in like-minded communities. Hanging out, messing around, and geeking out may sound like off-putting qualities, but they can open new doorways to access virtual Israel. Imagine the possibilities for shared communities of young Israeli and North American youth "hanging out" and talking about their day, their siblings, school work, parents, friends, love, loneliness, nothingness—and oh yes, also holidays and "Jewish stuff".

Language and Popular Culture

Studies in linguistics, culture studies, and identity suggest significant connections between the concepts of mind, self, society, and identity (Duranti 2004). The nascent Zionist movement was deeply rooted in the culturalist notion of the centrality of language to national aspirations and personal identity (Alter 1994; Schiff 1997). There are voices in the contemporary American Jewish life that bemoan the abandonment of a culture of spoken Hebrew in American Jewish life and education and its replacement with a "'ritual Hebrew" mainly taught for reading prayers or reciting bar/bat mitzvah portions (Sagarin 2015). Advocates of the Hebrew-as-culture approach cite instructive counter examples of Hebraic cultures in contemporary pre-schools, suburban public high schools in Chicago, day schools and community life in Latin-American countries, and in Jewish summer camps in mid-twentieth-century America (Mintz 1993). A new view of Hebrew might constitute an important cultural change for Israel education.

Music and art in pop culture are powerful resources for presenting the pulse and heartbeat of people (Toran 2015). They express voices, images, and stories in a way that speaks to the young and to people of all ages. Analysts of contemporary youth culture cite these spheres, particularly music, as the *lingua franca* of contemporary youth.[2] The use of visual art, literature, poetry, film, and the music of Israel provides educators with an accessible entry point to contemporary Israeli society and particularly to the world of its youth. Contemporary Israel is a veritable toy store of multiple forms of modern sounds, sights, foods, and people. This side of Israel has often been eclipsed by black and white newspaper photographs or 30-second television sound bites (which, indeed, are a part of contemporary Israel); however, even in the complicated reality called daily life in Israel, music, street life, attire, junk food, pop music, and graffiti connect one to the overall empire of contemporary youth (Glidden 2010).

Oeuvres and Rituals

Jerome Bruner cites the French cultural psychologist Ignace Meyerson who suggested that the main function of all collective cultural activity is to produce *oeuvres*—works (Bruner 1990). Meyerson's point was that cultures create objects or artifacts that reveal values and become expressions of core ideals. They help create communities, serve as sources of pride, and affirm values. *Oeuvres* encompass pop culture—the golden arches, or a half-eaten apple—as well as works of fine art and creativity; Meyerson believed that creating *oeuvres* and experiencing them were important for the young.

Rituals of Jewish life are important *oeuvres* of the Jewish people, and many of them have Israel woven into their fiber. For some, these *oeuvres* are divine commandment, and for others they are cultural mores; however, there is little doubt of their place in the Jewish mindset. These *oeuvres*, in fact, constitute a central preoccupation of most Jewish educational frameworks. However, the teaching of these rituals often does not overtly delineate their Israel-related motifs. The arks in synagogues typically face in the direction of Jerusalem, and many a young 13-year-old boy or 12-year-old girl has stood in the front of that ark on the day of their bar or bat mitzvah. The movie theater in a suburban neighborhood is likely to have a sign referring to an upcoming Israeli film festival. The Israeli basketball team plays exhibition games with NBA teams. These presences of Israel surface in the everyday life of the young, without always being apparent. Israeli artifacts are part of the general landscape, inhabited by a significant number of young North American Jews. These works are part of their "life space" even if not verbalized.

THE TRIP

The first trip to Israel was that of Abraham from the Land of Canaan. From that time on, Jews have been the quintessential travelers, and the trip to Israel has been the primal metaphor of the traveling trait (Johnson 1987). In the twentieth century, the metaphor became a reality as millions of Jews traveled to Israel to live there. With the establishment of the state, educational travel to Israel for youth from abroad began to increase, and by the 1980s it had become a dynamic, if relatively modest, form of informal Jewish education. By that time, the educational value of the Israel trip was recognized, as educators adapted the phrase "the Israel experience" to describe such educational travel for teens.[3] At the very end of the twentieth century, world Jewry and the State of Israel embarked on an effort called Birthright Israel to bring adolescents and young adults to Israel for an intensive ten-day educational program. (Saxe and Chazan 2008; Kellner 2012). This program was to constitute a major paradigm shift in American Jewish life, with more than half million young Jews having participated in a variegated program of Israel experience educational programs. Within a relatively short time, it is likely that for the first time since the destruction of the second Temple, the majority of the Jews of the world will have visited Israel. It is increasingly clear that one cannot conceive of an Israel education, which does not include an Israel experience. Indeed, if there is one facet of Israel education that has proven itself, it is that the power of an effective Israel experience is unmatched and irreplaceable.[4] It is only logical that Israel education without an experience in Israel at some point is only a partial activity.

The power of the actual experience in Israel is related, among other things, to Israel being a totally immersive culture. Embracing real-life experiences and the multiple expressions of Jewishness that exist both in Israel and in Jewish life today is paramount. Modern Israel encompasses the panorama of narratives from the biblical Promised Land to postmodern contemporary society that we discussed in Chap. 2. In Israel, Abraham, Moses, Hosea, Judah the Maccabee, Maimonides, Herzl, Ahad Ha'am, Golda Meir, and David Ben-Gurion are not only street names, but also figures who still "live" there and their "voices" are heard daily. Indeed, the Israeli experience provides a direct linkage to a rich heritage and a living culture. The power of this meeting is enhanced by being deeply experiential, sensual, and people-centered.

There are many ways to see Israel—with a *Fodor's©* *Guidebook*, a camera, the Bible, a prayer book, or the latest edition of *The New York Times*.[5] The person-centered approach obviously implies maximizing the direct encounter and minimizing mediated framings. It aims to facilitate a dialogue between person and place in which both speak to each other. Young travelers come to the Western Wall to speak to it, and the Wall wants to talk to them. The art of enabling encounter is a delicate one; sometimes in order to facilitate a direct interaction, it is necessary to engage in a certain degree of framing (or what is denoted as "pre-conditions of education") so that the encounter can actually happen. There are situations in which a totally unmediated dynamic can sometimes actually prevent, rather than enable, genuine experience. The art of framing is the ability to enable the dialogue to take place, and not to impose a specific landscape on the actual moment. The actual implementation of Israel trips is a fine art, which has proven to be one of the unique achievements of American Jewish education. Indeed, one might well suggest that this aspect has been one of the most professional and sophisticated of contemporary forms of Jewish education.

RELATING AND RELATIONSHIPS

The emergence of the field of Israel educational travel was accompanied by diverse pedagogies and methodologies. One of the more creative innovations in the field was pioneered by a young Jewish educator named Anne Lanski, who believed that visiting Israel was more than seeing ancient arches or tombs. It also (and, perhaps, mainly) involved interacting with real people who laugh, cry, and talk. Her thinking was initially encapsulated in the Hebrew word *mifgash* which literally means "meeting" and was used to refer to interactive programming between Israeli and overseas youth as part of the Israel experience. Over time, and particularly with the advent of Birthright Israel, *mifgash* became a fairly mainstream component of educational travel. On Birthright Israel trips, Israeli participants spend 5–10 days of the 10-day birthright trip as equal participants (Saxe and Chazan 2008). At a certain point, Lanski felt that while the *mifgash* idea was powerful, it had become too linked to being understood as a "program" rather than as an educational and heuristic process (Lanski et al. 2015). Consequently, Lanski and colleagues have expanded their original thinking of encounter into a prioritization of what they now call "relating and relationships" which they define as building meaningful and lasting interactions that become the connections that sustain, nurture, and enrich us individually and collectively. They suggest that the relationship building process begins and ends with the participants and their inner world, and then moves toward the collective. This practical pedagogy reflects a language of the dialogical that Martin Buber was to use in the twentieth-century theology and education. Buber used such phrases as "all real life is meeting" and "all actual life is an encounter" (Buber 1958). In terms of the Israel experience, this dialogic approach suggested the perspective of Israel rooted not only in holy sites or historical ruins, but also on normal people buying fruits and vegetables for their family.[6]

THE EDUCATOR

For many people, the educator is the key factor in education. Whether one accepts this generalization or not, it is clear that educators play a central role in the elaborate process of Israel education that we have described in the previous two chapters. Indeed, our past discussions point to certain core values, aptitudes, and tasks of an Israeli educator.

The first necessary skill set is relationship building—the ability to be a connector between the student and the idea of Israel. This task is a process that encompasses listening skills that make the student feel comfortable to speak, questioning skills that are aimed at initiating conversation, sensitivity skills that create a comfortable personal and group setting, and the personal trait of humility (what David Brooks calls "epistemological modesty" (Brooks 1999).

A second skill set is facilitation of discussion between the student and texts which constitute Land of Israel narratives. These texts need to be studied in a way that makes their analysis and deconstruction communicative to the student and helps him/her internalize their diverse meanings. This skill set requires familiarity with core texts and the ability to guide students through a careful literal and then interpretive reading and discussion of the positions presented in these texts. The orientation of the educator in this instance is personalization, meaning-making, and big ideas, and, in this instance, is less focused on *halakhic*, and decoding skills (Holtz; and Levisohn 2013).

A third skill set is an approach to Jewish rituals—prayer, holidays, home observance, grace after meals—which, among other foci, helps the young discover the pervasive Israeli presence in these areas of Jewish life. A core blessing in the grace after meals refers to the rebuilding of Jerusalem. The prayer cited when the Torah scroll is removed from the ark announces that the Torah "came forth from Zion, and the word of Lord from Jerusalem" (Isaiah 2:3). At the end of a wedding ceremony, a glass is broken by the groom as a remembrance of the fallen Temple in Jerusalem. These rituals are both moments of piety and manifestation of the presence of Israel in everyday Jewish life.

The fourth skill set is what we have in this chapter called culture building. The pedagogy of culture building includes understanding and structuring of physical space, use of music and art, literature Israeli peers, travel to Israel posters, and regalia of Israel. This skill set is rooted in general cultural sensibility and sensitivity which, while having specific Israeli content, has elements of the mindsets and perspectives of a Steven Spielberg, Zubin Mehta, and *Cirque du Soleil.*

All of these are critical, but the key skill set of the Israel educator is actually none of these. It is about something much deeper which is at the core. It is about the relationship within or the landscape of the teacher's inner soul. This vision belongs to Parker Palmer—a shaping contemporary figure in advocating for the primacy of the teacher in a human-focused education. Palmer's life work speaks directly to our discussion of Israel education. He begins with the notion of the inner landscape of the teacher's soul which he regards as the starting point and fulcrum of pedagogy. He speaks about the courage needed to teach from within—of teaching from that spot where mind and heart come together to shape a total human being. For Palmer, teaching is not about the "what" or the "how" of education; rather, it is about the "why" and the "who". His chief pedagogic tool is the heart of a teacher—and the identity and integrity which the teacher utilizes in his or her work. In contrast to some approaches to teaching which call for the distancing of self from the teaching content and act, Palmer says that this is where teaching begins. Teaching is not about transmission of facts—we have computers that can do that. It is rather about the re-shaping of character—and there is no technology that do that. How one learns about good character is by being near people of positive character. Palmer's teacher is not a preacher who "transmits", but an instructor who feels, thinks, questions, achieves, and sometimes fails—all of which are traits of character. Palmer's teacher is a living breathing human being who utilizes the totality of mind and heart as his core pedagogical technique.

There is probably is no topic that is more fitting for a Palmer teacher than Israel.[7] Israel education calls for educators who model commitment, thinking, feeling, doubt, questioning, joy, sadness, certainty, and epistemological modesty. A subject as beloved, complicated, engaging, and confusing as Israel deserves a Parker Palmer teacher. Being an Israel educator has sometimes been regarded as a complicated endeavor in this period of the contemporary State of Israel.[8] The establishment and achievements of the contemporary state are observable. Its importance for world Jewry is palpable. However, some dynamics related to contemporary Israel, such as the geo-political conflict, religion and democracy, and the use of power have become problematic issues for educators. Ultimately, the issue is not specific to Israel education; it is about the challenge of teaching topics, places, and histories that are fraught with value complexity. The Bible is a document of great majesty; yet, there are sections that are fraught not just with moral dilemmas but also with instances of moral behaviors, which seem incomprehensible. This dilemma is not limited to parochial education. The teachings of American history encompass grand moments of core American values and at the same significant examples of moral deficiency (Ragland and Woestman, 2009).

The answer to the issue of teaching a topic which includes ambiguity for the teacher, returns to our discussion in chapters 1 and 2: what is the aim, what is the subject, and what kind of education is Israel education? The aim of Israel education is relationship; the subject is the person; and the domain is value education. Whether one is teaching American history, ethnic heritage, or contemporary Israel, one has entered arenas that are about values and value choices. Ours is not to preach the right or the wrong; it is to develop the ability to negotiate the complex landscape known as life. The ability to negotiate this landscape is one the core missions of education; it is in this sense that Palmer speaks about the courage to teach. The challenge raised in the contemporary discussion of Israel is about the larger issues of conflict and decisions. The world in which we live includes dissonance and conflict. The cultures we live in do not fit together like the perfect jigsaw puzzle. There are sometimes pieces that take a long time to put in the right spot; sometimes pieces get lost; sometimes you just don't have any more patience and you break up the pieces out of frustration—or pleasure. Our task in Israel education is very much related to helping our charges through the deeply engaging, and also periodically complicating, pathways that constitute an Israeli relationship. This task encompasses dealing with difficult issues in a way that is developmentally appropriate, while also allowing voices of assent and dissent to be heard. One of the virtues of contemporary Israeli life is the presence of diverse voices, and they should find their place in the life and education of our young at the opportune moments. Our task as educators is to be passionate about a culture of open dialogue of diverse opinions, policies, and perspectives. One of the ways that a person learns to be a choosing person is by being around people and educational settings that teach us that choice exists and how to deal with it. The pathways of Israel, old and new, are lined with past treasures and contemporary achievement, and along the way there have been, are, and always will be diverse side roads and sometimes even dead ends. Twenty-first-century life includes complexity and nuance. This is not a position of compromise or weakness or of compliance; this is the culture of the will to educate.

THE WOVEN TAPESTRY

In these three chapters we have attempted to present a logical, clearly defined and articulated pattern approach to the contemporary topic of Israel education. But, truth be told, our tasks ultimately is that of the weaver. Our task encompasses presenting a vision, proposing an educational aim, delineating specific contents, proposing methodologies, creating cultures, and describing the role of the educator. The ultimate task is about weaving together a host of threads, some of which flow smoothly and some of which do not seem to connect. Durkheim exaggerated when he implied that educators are superheroes and so did Nietzsche and Freud when they indicated that ours is an impossible profession (Durkheim 1956; Nietzsche 2015; Britzman 2009). We are probably best seen as weavers of a tapestry, hosts of a well-orchestrated party of diverse guests, and master conductors of a symphony. Our mission is to enable the music of education to win out over the din of postmodern life.

BIBLIOGRAPHY

Alter, R. (1994). *Hebrew and modernity*. Bloomington: Indiana University Press. Print.

Bettelheim, Bruno. (1950). *Love is Not Enough*. Chicago: Free Press. Print.

Britzman, D. P. (2009). *The very thought of education: Psychoanalysis and the impossible professions*. Albany: State University of New York. Print.

Brooks, D. (1999). *The social animal: The hidden sources of love, character, and achievement*. New York: Random House, 2012. Print.

Brooks, David. (2011). *The Social Animal: The Hidden Sources of Love, Character, and Achievement*. New York: Random House. Print

Bruner, Jerome. (1997). *The Culture of Education*. Cambridge: Harvard UP. Print.

Bruner, J. (1990). *The culture of education*. Cambridge, MA: Harvard University Press, 1996. Print.

Buber, M. (1958). *I and thou*. New York: Charles Scribner and Sons, 1970. Print.

Christakis, N. A., & Fowler, J. H. (2009). *Connected: The surprising power of our social networks and how they shape our lives*. New York: Little, Brown. Print.

Duranti, Alessandro. (1997). *Linguistic Anthropology*. Cambridge: Cambridge University Press. Print.

Duranti, A. (2004). *Linguistic anthropology*. New York: Cambridge University Press, 1997. Print.

Durkheim, É. (1956). *Education and sociology*. Glencoe: Free Press. Print.

Eto, Mizuko. (2009). *Hanging Out, Messing Around, and Geeking Out*. Cambridge: MIT Press. Print.

Freud, S. (1962). *Civilization and its discontents*. New York: W.W. Norton. Print.

Glidden, Sarah and Clem Robins. (2010). *How to Understand Israel in 60 Days or Less*. New York: Vertigo/DC Comics. Print.

Goffman, E. (1960). *Asylums: Essays on the social situation of mental patients and other inmates*. New York: Anchor Books, 1961, Print.

Goffman, Erving. (1961). *Asylums: Essays on the Social Situation of Mental Patients and Other Inmates.* New York: Anchor Books. Print.

Goitein, S. D. (1999). *A Mediterranean society.* Berkeley: University of California Press.

Holtz, B. (2013). A map of orientations to the teaching of Bible. In J. Levisohn, & S. Fendrick (Eds.), *Turn it and turn it again: Studies in the etching and learning of classical Jewish texts.* Boston: Academic studies Press, 2023. Print.

Ito, M. (2011). *Hanging out, messing around, and geeking out; Kids learning and living with new media.* Cambridge, MA: MIT, 2010. Print.

Johnson, P. (1987). *A history of the Jews.* New York: Harper & Row. Print.

Lanski, A., Stewart, A., & Werchow, Y. (2015). Relating and relationships. *The Aleph Bets of Israel education.* N. pag. www.theicenter.org. The iCenter for Israel Education. Web.

Levisohn, J. (2013). What are the orientations to the teaching of Rabbinic literature? In *Turn it and turn it again: Studies in the teaching and learning of classical texts.* Boston: Academic Studies Press. Print.

Levisohn, Jon and Fendrick, Susan, editors. (2014). *Turn It and Turn It Again: Studies in the Teaching and Learning of Clasisical Jewish Texts.* Boston: Academic Studies Press. Print.

Mintz, A. L. (1993). *Hebrew in America: Perspectives and prospects.* Detroit: Wayne State University Press. Print.

Neill, A. S. (1970). *Summerhill: For & against.* New York: Hart Pub. Print.

Nietzsche, Friedrich. (2015). *Anti-Education: On the Future of Our Educational Institutions.* New York: NYRB Classics. Print.

Peshkin, A. (1986). *God's choice: The total world of a fundamentalist Christian school.* Chicago: University of Chicago. Print.

Redl, F., & Wineman, D. (1957). *The aggressive child.* Glencoe: Free. Print.

Sagarin, Lori. (2015). Modern Hebrew: Culture and Identity. *The Alef Bet of Israel education.* N. pag. www.theicenter.org. The iCenter for Israel Education. Web.

Sartre, J.-P. (1967). *Existentialism and human emotions.* New York: Philosophical Library. Print.

Saxe, L., & Chazan, B. I. (2008). *Ten days of birthright Israel: A journey in young adult identity.* Waltham: Brandeis University Press. Print.

Schiff, Alvin. (1997). *The Mystique of Hebrew.* New York: Schreiber, Shengold Publishing. Print.

Soberman, M., & Stewart, A. (2015). Experiencing Israel. In *The Aleph Bet of Israel education.* The iCenter Press: Northbrook. Print.

Thomas, D., & Brown, J. S. (2011). *A new culture of learning: Cultivating the imagination for a world of constant change.* Lexington: CreateSpace. Print.

Toran, Vavi. (2015). Israeli Arts and Culture: the Ability to Engage. *The Alef Bet of Israel education.* N. pag. www.theicenter.org. The iCenter for Israel Education. Web.

Notes

1. Some of these institutions are Bettelheim's Sonia Shankman Orthogenic School in Chicago, Redl and Wineman's Pioneer House in Detroit, Neil's Summerhill, and Peskin's Bethany Academy.

2. "The shift from stuff to experiences has had a profound impact on the soundtrack of Youth of the nation, as the popular center of gravity has seemingly shifted. Hip-hop, largely focused on messages of affluence and excess, is giving way to tech-fueled electronic dance material (EDM), largely rooted in experiences, love, and relationships—in some ways coming full circle to the sixties generation, but with a much different look and sound" (p. 37) (Matt Britton. *YOUTH NATION: Building Remarkable Brands in a Youth-Driven Culture*. New York: Wiley, 2015).

3. In the last decades of the twentieth century, the educational trip to Israel has become known by the generic name "The Israel experience", reflecting an attempt to link this activity to John Dewey's ideas on experience and education, and this nomenclature entered the vocabulary of Jewish education. See: David Bryfman, editor. *Experience and Jewish Education*, Los Angeles Torah Aura, 2014.

4. There has been extensive research on Israel education over the past two decades. See Eric Cohen, *Youth Tourism to Israel: Educational Experiences of the Diaspora* (*Channel View Publications, 2008*). *The Israeli Experience*; Leonard Saxe et al. Birthright Israel (op. cit). Research on Israel in Jewish Education, Berman Center of Research, New York University.

5. The Israeli poet Yehuda Amichai wrote "he who loves Jerusalem by the tourist book or the prayer book is like one who loves a woman by a manual of sex positions" (*Love of Jerusalem*, Yehuda Amichai. *Collected Poetry*, New York: Harper and Row, 1988).

6. A poignant example of a thwarted encounter may be found in two autobiographies written on two sides of the same fence. One is the book *Once Upon a Country* by Palestinian intellectual Sari Nusseibeh, and the other is the book *A Tale of Love and Darkness* by Israeli writer Amos Oz. Both write almost identical books about childhood and youth, alleyways, people, and nostalgically growing up in Israel—one in Palestinian East Jerusalem and the other in Jewish West Jerusalem.

7. Parker Palmer's work has extended to an interest in issues related to the subject of this book. He has written an important Prelude to the *Aleph Bet of Israel Education, 2nd Edition*, which has been published by the iCenter for Israel Education (Professor Lee Shulman, former head of the Carnegie Foundation, and Professor Emeritus of Stanford University have written an equally engaging postlude).

8. Two books that explore these complexities are *Loving Israel: an Educational Guide for Liberal Zionism* by Alex Sinclair and *Israel Matters* by Lisa Grant and Ezra Kopelowitz. Grant and Kopelowitz use the word "matters" to refer both to the noun "matters" meaning things or situations and to the verb "matters" meaning it is important or it is something we care about (Lisa Grant and Ezra Kopelowitz, *Israel Matters: A 21st Century Paradigm for Jewish Education*, Jerusalem: Center for Peoplehood Education, 2012).

4

Epilogue

Abstract The analysis of Israel in Jewish education is a lens for reflecting on the relationship between ethnic education and ethical education. It sometimes is the case that through our particularity we find our humanity. Particularistic education might also encompass education for a life of values, character, and benevolence. Such education requires faith in people and their journeys through the texts, history, and events of their own culture and also of other cultures.

Keywords Dialogical • Humanitas • Hebrew Humanism • Liberal learning

Homeland and Humanitas

This book has focused on the place of Israel in contemporary Jewish education. It has proposed a philosophy of Israel education rooted in the personal relationship between contemporary youth and the value of the Land of Israel. This educational vision implies a pedagogy of direct conversations between the young and core voices and texts of the Land of Israel and the contemporary State of Israel. These texts and voices point to the ongoing commitment of the Jewish people to the value of Israel over time, as well as to the diversity of meanings of the value of Israel. This educational approach to Israel education is understood as value education, which

© The Author(s) 2016
B. Chazan, *A Philosophy of Israel Education*,
DOI 10.1007/978-3-319-30779-4_4

means that ultimately it is aimed at the development of personal character. In this epilogue, we reflect on implications of this study beyond the Jewish sphere. The presenting question is "Can an education that focuses on a specific ethnic or affiliative group also be a framework for character education?"

FROM ETHNIC TO ETHIC

Our approach to Israel education reflects some core understandings of the concept of education. We regard the individual as the main focus of education. This focus does not negate the importance of social identities in shaping who we are. However, ultimately education is about the personal journey to becoming human. This person-centered approach is particularly significant in our postmodern world of multiple identities and voluntary affiliations; it reflects the long-standing tradition of humanistic education which regards the goal of education to be how to be human or how to live a good life. The process of choosing values is not haphazard or casual; rather, it is a reflective process, which is ignited by the passion to seek and find a meaningful set of values for one's life. Our study of Israel education suggests that the gateway to meeting these values is through the diverse texts and documents of a tradition. We learn about a tradition's values by studying its "personal diary"—the records of what it professes to believe and what it becomes in practice. Indeed, the values of nations and peoples are recorded both in documents and equally in the norms and practices of its daily life. The ultimate confrontation with values is the dialogical confrontation between the individual and these written and lived testimonies.

What are the implications of these emphases for the challenge of transforming ethnic education into ethical education? First, the person, and not the ethnos, is the center of education. Second, such education encourages reflection on values that are posited, rather than on conclusions to be imposed. Third, education's role is to help students learn how to choose and not to abandon them to whim or other-directedness. Fourth, education for values is not a subject to be studied only in the abstract. The measure of the values of a people, a nation, or a culture is both their theoretical suppositions and their implementation in practice. Fifth, the existence of multiple values does not mean that values are ultimately personal, parochial, or arbitrary. Values must stand the test of reason, insight, and universalizability. Finally, the quest for values is about the search for ideals that know no national borders and that are applicable for people regardless of their voluntary or involuntary affiliations.

An important teacher of this educational vision is the twentieth-century German-Jewish philosopher Martin Buber.[1] Buber utilized the phrase "Hebrew Humanism" to refer to a worldview which he believed synthesized the great Hebraic and humanistic traditions in a compelling way. His understanding of the humanistic or humanitas is "the belief that man is not merely a zoological species, but a unique creature" whose lot it is to seek and find the inherently human in his/her self[2] (Buber 1941). The "Hebrew" part of his phrase refers to the specific ethos of the Jewish people whose source is the Bible, "which divides right from wrong, truth from lies, as unconditionally as the words of the Creator divided light from darkness" (p. 162, *op cit.*). Hebrew humanism is a synthesis of these two visions, which is both a philosophical concept and an action plan for a Jewish homeland. Buber was a supporter and active participant of that enterprise. At the same time, he was insistent on warning new and old nations of the misguided and egotistical tendency of nation states to forget the person and to deify the state.

Toward a New Ethnic Educational Vision

We believe that, under the right conditions, particularistic education can be a significant force in education for a life of values, character, and benevolence. Indeed, it is often the case that through our particularity we find our humanity. Such education requires faith in people and their journeys through the texts, history, and events of their own culture and also of other cultures. The journey to the "State of Humanitas" is ongoing, confusing, invigorating, and thought-provoking. It is our mission and calling as educators to serve as guides, mentors, and partners of the young on this journey. Our contemporary world, at times, appears as if "things fall apart; the center cannot hold and mere anarchy is loosed upon the world" (Yeats 1950). Perhaps, we can help our young of diverse affiliations and identities to yet meet together in the State of Humanitas.

Bibliography

Yeats, W. B. (1950). *The collected poems of W.B. Yeats.* London: Macmillan. Print.

Notes

1. Martin Buber was born in 1878 in Vienna and died in 1965 in Jerusalem. He was a professor and activist of Jewish communal affairs in Germany until 1938 when he immigrated to Palestine and served as a professor at Hebrew University of Jerusalem. His major works on education include *Teaching and the Deed, On National Education, "Education"* and *Education of Character*. Essays related to Hebrew humanism include "Hebrew Humanism", "Nationalism", "Biblical humanism" and "Zionism and Nationalism".

2. Buber's term "humanitas" is related to the term "liberal learning" used by British philosopher Michael Oakeshott to refer to the search for the core values that make each of us human. Oakeshott saw learning as an ongoing adventure and journey in exploring, observing, and choosing values of worth that shape our lives and human society. The travelers in this journey engage in conversations with works of art, literature, philosophy, and architecture, which help them over time to understand what it means to be human. This education is denoted as liberal.

Bibliography

(1948). *The declaration of independence of the State of Israel.* N.p.: Israel Office. Web.

"A portrait of Jewish Americans" (2013, September 30). N.p. Web.

Ackerman, W. (1969). Jewish education-for what? *American Jewish Yearbook.* N. pag. Web.

Aichhorn, A. (1962). *Wayward youth: A psychoanalytic study of delinquent children: Illustrated by actual case histories.* Cleveland: World Pub. Print.

Amichai, Y., & Harshav, B. (1994). *A life of poetry: 1948–1994.* New York: HarperCollins. Print.

Aristotle, & Ross, W. D. (1966). *The works of Aristotle.* London: Oxford University Press. Print.

Armstrong, K. (2000). *Islam: A short history.* New York: Modern Library. Print.

Art, B. (1993). *What is the best life? An introduction to ethics.* Belmont: Wadsworth Publishing Co. Print.

Banks, J., & Banks, C. A. M. (2013). *Multicultural education: Issues and perspectives.* New York: Wiley. Print

Beinart, P. (2012). *The crisis of Zionism.* New York: Times/Henry Holt. Print.

Bialik, H., & Ravnitsky, Y. (1992). *The book of legends. Sefer Ha-Aggadah.* New York: Schocken. Print.

Biemann, A. (Ed.). (2002). *The Martin Buber reader.* New York: Palgrave MacMillan. N. pag. Print.

Block, A. A. (2004). *Talmud, curriculum, and the practical: Joseph Schwab and the Rabbis.* New York: P. Lang. Print.

Boman, T. (1954). *Hebrew thought compared with Greek.* Philadelphia: Westminster. Print.

© The Author(s) 2016

B. Chazan, *A Philosophy of Israel Education,*

DOI 10.1007/978-3-319-30779-4

Boyd, D., & Goldenberg, J. (2014). *Inside the box: A proven system of creativity for breakthrough results.* New York: Simon and Shuster. Print.

Brooks, D. (2011). *The social animal: The hidden sources of love, character, and achievement.* New York: Random House. Print.

Bruner, J. S. (1997). *The culture of education.* Cambridge, MA: Harvard University Press. Print.

Buber, M. (1937). *I and thou.* (trans: Kaufmann, W.). New York: Charles. N. pag. Print.

Buber, M. (1947a). Education. In *Between man and man.* London: Fontana Library. N. pag. Print.

Buber, M. (1947b). The education of character. In *Between man and man.* London: Fontana Library. N. pag. Print.

Buber, M. (1948). On national education. In *Israel and the world.* New York: Schocken. N. pag. Print.

Buber, M. (2002a). Biblical humanism. In A. Biemann (Ed.), *The Martin Buber reader.* New York: Palgrave MacMillan. N. pag. Print.

Buber, M. (2002b). Hebrew humanism. In *The Martin Buber reader.* New York: Palgrave MacMillan. N. pag. Print.

Buber, M. (2002c). Teaching and deed. In A. Biemann (Ed.), *The Martin Buber reader.* New York: Palgrave MacMillan. N. pag. Print.

Buber, M., & Smith, R. G. (1949). *Between man and man.* London: Routledge & Paul. Print.

Chazan, B. (1978). *The language of Jewish education: Crisis and hope in the Jewish school.* New York: Hartmore House. Print.

Chazan, Barry (2015). A Linguistic analysis of the role of Israel in American Jewish Schooling. *Journal of Jewish Education*, 81,1, 2015)

Cohen, J. (2014). Carrying the past into the future: Texts and teaching in contemporary Jewish education. Jerusalem: Hebrew University of Jerusalem. Lecture.

Cohen, J. (1999). Hermeneutic options for the teaching of canonical texts: Freud, Fromm, Strauss, and Buber read the Bible. *Crossroads.* N. pag. Web.

Cremin, L. A. (1976). *Public education.* New York: Basic. Print.

Cremin, Lawrence (1988). *American Education: the Metropolitan Experience, 1876–1980.* New York: Harpercollins. Print.

Daniels, H., Cole, M., & Wertsch, J. V. (2007). *The Cambridge companion to Vygotsky.* Cambridge, MA: Cambridge University Press. Print.

Deboer, M. J., & Elazar, D. J. (2001). Covenant and polity in Biblical Israel: Biblical foundations & Jewish expressions. *Journal of Law and Religion, 16*(2), 805. Web.

Dewey, J. (1910). *How we think.* Boston: D.C. Heath. Print.

Dewey, J. (1916). *Democracy and education: An introduction to the philosophy of education.* New York: Macmillan. Print.

Dewey, J. (1930). *Human nature and conduct: An introduction to social psychology.* New York: Modern Library. Print.

Dewey, J. (1959). *Moral principles in education.* New York: Philosophical Library. Print.

Dimitrovsky, Z. (1976). *Exploring the Talmud. Volume 1. Education.* New York: Ktav House. Print.

Donoghue, D. (1998). *The practice of reading.* New Haven: Yale University Press. Print.

Dow, P. (2013). *Virtuous minds: Intellectual character development for students, educators, & parents.* Downers Grove: InterVarsity. Print.

Dresner, S. (Ed.). (1992). *I asked for wonder: A spiritual anthology of Abraham Joshua Heschel.* New York: Crossroad. Print.

Eisenstein, S., & Grotjahn, M. (n.d.). Siegfried Bernfeld, 1892–1953. In F. Alexander (Ed.), *Psychoanalytic Pioneers.* New York: Basic, N. page. Print.

Erikson, E. H. (1964). *Childhood and society.* New York: Norton. Print.

Erikson, E. H., & Erikson, J. M. (1997). *The life cycle completed.* New York: W.W. Norton. Print.

Fraenkel, C., & Walzer, M. (2015). *Teaching Plato in Palestine; foreword by Michael Walzer: Philosophy in a divided world.* Princeton: Princeton University Press. Print.

Frankl, V. E. (1964). *Man's search for meaning: An introduction to logotherapy.* London: Hodder and Stoughton. Print.

Gay, P. (1987). *A Godless Jew: Freud, atheism, and the making of psychoanalysis.* New Haven: Yale University Press. Print.

Glidden, S., & Robins, C. (2010). *How to understand Israel in 60 days or less.* New York: Vertigo/DC Comics. Print.

Grant, L. D., & Kopelowitz, E. (2012). *Israel education matters: 21st century paradigm for Jewish education.* Jerusalem: Center for Jewish Peoplehood Education. Print.

Handelman, S. A. (1982a). *The slayers of Moses: The emergence of rabbinic interpretation in modern literary theory.* Albany: State University of New York Press. Print.

Handelman, S. A. (2011). *Make yourself a teacher: Rabbinic tales of mentors and disciples.* Seattle: University of Washington. Print.

Hare, R. M. (1964). *The language of morals.* New York: Oxford University Press. Print.

Haroutunian-Gordon, S. (1991). *Learning to teach through discussion: The art of turning the soul.* New Haven: Yale University Press. Print.

Headenver.org/rabbigruenwald2010/02/06/standing-at-sinai. (n.d.) N.p. Web.

Heilman, S. C. (1995). *Portrait of American Jews: The last half of the 20th century.* Seattle: University of Washington. Print.

Herberg, W. (1983). *An essay in American religious sociology: Protestant-Catholic-Jew.* Chicago: University of Chicago Press.

Herzl, T., & Lowenthal, M. (1956). *The diaries of Theodor Herzl.* New York: Dial. Print.

Heschel, A. J., & Dresner, S. H. (1983). *I asked for wonder: A spiritual anthology.* New York: Crossroad. Print.

Hollinger, D. A. (1995). *Post ethnic America: Beyond multiculturalism.* New York: Basic. Print.

Holzer, E., & Kent, O. (2013). *A philosophy of Havruta: Understanding and teaching the art of text study in pairs.* Boston: Academic Studies. Print.

Ito, M. (2010). *Hanging out, messing around, and geeking out: Kids living and learning with new media.* Cambridge, MA: MIT. Print.

Jaeger, W., & Highest, G. (1986). *Paideia: The ideals of Greek culture.* New York: Oxford University Press. Print.

Kadushin, M. (1952). *The rabbinic mind.* New York: Jewish Theological Seminary of America. Print.

Kohlberg, L. (1981a). *Essays on moral development/the philosophy of moral development: Moral stages and the idea of justice.* San Francisco: Harper & Row. Print.

Kohlberg, L. (1981b). *The philosophy of moral development: Moral stages and the idea of justice.* San Francisco: Harper & Row. Print.

Krasner, J. (2011). *The Benderly boys and American Jewish education.* Waltham: Brandeis University Press. Print.

Levisohn, J. (n.d.). http://ejewishphilanthropy.com/what-we-know-about-jewish-identity. N.p. Web.

Levisohn, J. A., & Fendrick, S. P. (2013). *Turn it and turn it again: Studies in the teaching and learning of classical Jewish texts.* Boston: Academic Studies. Print.

Marrou, H. I. (1964). *A history of education in antiquity.* New York: New American Library. Print.

Matthews, G. B. (1980). *Philosophy and the young child.* Cambridge, MA: Harvard University Press. Print.

Munsey, B. (1980). *Moral development, moral education, and Kohlberg: Basic issues in philosophy, psychology, religion, and education.* Birmingham: Religious Education. Print.

Nusseibeh, S., & David, A. (2007). *Once upon a country: A Palestinian life.* New York: Farrar, Straus and Giroux. Print.

Oz, A. (2004). *A tale of love and darkness.* Orlando: Harcourt. Print.

Oz, A., & Oz-Salberger, F. (2012). *Jews and words.* New Haven: Yale University Press. Print.

Parks, S. (2011). *Big questions, worthy dreams: Mentoring emerging adults in their search for meaning, purpose, and faith.* San Francisco: Jossey-Bass. Print.

Perkins, D. N. (2009). *Making learning whole: How seven principles of teaching can transform education.* San Francisco: Jossey-Bass. Print.

Perkins, D. N. (2014). *Future-wise.* San Francisco: Jossey-Bass. Print.

Peters, R. S. (1967). *Ethics and education.* Atlanta: Foresman. Print.

Peters, R. S. (1981). *Moral development and moral education.* London: G. Allen & Unwin. Print.

Phillips, C. (2004). *Six questions of Socrates: A modern-day journey of discovery through world philosophy*. New York: W.W. Norton. Print.

Pinar, W. F. (1995). *Understanding curriculum: An introduction to the study of historical and contemporary curriculum discourses*. New York: P. Lang. Print.

Pinar, W. (2013). *Curriculum studies in the United States*. New York: Palgrave Pivot. Web.

Pomson, A., & Deitcher, H. (2009). *Jewish day schools, Jewish communities: A reconsideration*. Oxford: Littman Library of Jewish Civilization. Print.

Rubinstein, E. (1998). The declaration of independence as a basic document of the State of Israel. *Israel Studies, 3*(1), 195–210. Web.

Sacks, O. (1995). *An anthropologist on Mars: Seven paradoxical tales*. New York: Alfred A. Knopf. Print.

Said, E. W. (1992). *The question of Palestine*. New York: Vintage. Print.

Scheffler, I. (n.d.). The language of education. N.p. Web.

Scholes, R. (1985). *Textual power: Literary theory and the teaching of English*. New Haven: Yale University Press. Print.

Shama, S. (1995). *Landscape and memory*. New York: Simon and Shuster. Print.

Tillich, P. (1958). *Dynamics of faith*. New York: Harper. Print.

Uris, L. (1958). *Exodus*. Garden City: Doubleday. Print.

Wertheimer, J. (2009). *Learning and community: Jewish supplementary schools in the twenty-first century*. Waltham: Brandeis University Press. Print.

Westbrook, R. B. (1991). *John Dewey and American democracy*. Ithaca: Cornell University Press. Print.

Wieseltier, L. (1996). *Against identity*. New York: W. Drenttel. Print.

Wilson, E. O. (1998). *Consilience: The unity of knowledge*. New York: Alfred A. Knopf. Print.

Woocher, J. (2011, August 18). *eJewishphilanthropy*. N.p. Web.

www.aish.com/j/h/cc/48932202.htm?tab=y. (n.d.). N.p. Web.

www.ctc.ca.gov/credentials/CREDS. (n.d.). N.p. Web.

Zagzebski, L. (1996). *Virtues of the mind: An inquiry into the nature of virtue and ethical foundations of knowledge*. Cambridge, MA: Cambridge University Press. Print.

INDEX

© The Author(s) 2016
B. Chazan, *A Philosophy of Israel Education*,
DOI 10.1007/978-3-319-30779-4